# Words of Praise for
## *No Cape Required*

"You don't need a cape to become the hero God created you to be. All you need is the inspiration, some prayer, and an action plan. In this marvelous little book, Kristen Parrish provides all three. Read it and become a superhero to those around you!"

> — Michael Hyatt, *New York Times* best-
> selling author; former CEO, Thomas
> Nelson Publishers

"Just when I thought it was impossible to find a devotional that was biblically strong and creatively relevant—*Ka-Pow!*—along came *No Cape Required*. My entire family loves it and it's fueled some really great discussions. Thanks Kristen, we all give it five stars!"

> — Phil Joel and family, CCM
> recording artist and founder of
> deliberatePeople and deliberateKids
> music and ministries

"Kristen has written a beautiful, extremely practical devotional that I know will bless you all emphatically."

> — from the foreword by Jefferson
> Bethke, author of *Jesus > Religion*

"Who would have thought that Indiana Jones, Huck Finn, and Zorro could teach us so much about faith? In *No Cape Required*, Kristen Parrish shows us amazing parallels between the heroes of our culture and the God-inspired inner hero in each of us. It _____ of Christianity and the real world. Best of all, _____ ad inside all along. Step aside, Captain

> _____ *imes* best-
> orian

"From Andy Griffith to Zorro, Kristen Parrish mines literature and movies for bite-sized biblical lessons. *No Cape Required* puts the fun in profundity. Fifty-two thumbs up!"

— Bob Welch, author of *52 Little Lessons from Les Miserables*

"In her latest book, *No Cape Required*, Kristen Parrish encourages and instructs, charms and persuades, and with a text that almost seems weightless. This is not an easy thing for any writer to achieve, and Parrish has done it, with or without cape. Using our favorite characters from film, literature, television, and comics, Parrish has crafted a devotional masterpiece. This is hardly an exaggeration. Her wit sparkles. I found this a difficult book to put down."

— David Teems, author of *Majestie: The King Behind the King James Bible* and *Tyndale: The Man Who Gave God an English Voice*

"*No Cape Required* brought me encouragement, strength, and peace while going through a hard time. These easy-to-read, short devotions are great for youth and small group settings. The modern and classic stories cleverly woven together with Scripture bring a relevant and needed edge to Western culture."

— Roddy MacIvor, public speaker and youth pastor

# NO CAPE
# REQUIRED

A DEVOTIONAL

**52 WAYS TO UNLEASH YOUR INNER HERO**

# KRISTEN PARRISH

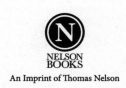

NELSON
BOOKS

An Imprint of Thomas Nelson

Published in Nashville, Tennessee, by Nelson Books, an imprint of Thomas Nelson. Nelson Books and Thomas Nelson are registered trademarks of HarperCollins Christian Publishing, Inc.

Thomas Nelson, Inc., titles may be purchased in bulk for educational, business, fund-raising, or sales promotional use. For information, please e-mail SpecialMarkets@ThomasNelson.com.

Unless otherwise indicated, Scripture quotations are taken from the NEW KING JAMES VERSION. © 1982 by Thomas Nelson, Inc. Used by permission. All rights reserved.

Scripture quotations marked ESV are taken from THE ENGLISH STANDARD VERSION. © 2001 by Crossway Bibles, a division of Good News Publishers.

Scripture quotations marked KJV are taken from the Holy Bible, King James Version (public domain).

Scripture quotations marked NIV are taken from the Holy Bible, New International Version®, NIV®. Copyright © 1973, 1978, 1984, 2011 by Biblica, Inc.™ Used by permission of Zondervan. All rights reserved worldwide. www.zondervan.com.

Scripture quotations marked NLT are taken from Holy Bible, New Living Translation. © 1996, 2004, 2007. Used by permission of Tyndale House Publishers, Inc., Carol Stream, Illinois 60188. All rights reserved.

Scripture quotations marked NRSV are taken from the NEW REVISED STANDARD VERSION of the Bible. © 1989 by the Division of Christian Education of the National Council of the Churches of Christ in the U.S.A. All rights reserved.

Scripture quotations marked MSG are taken from The Message by Eugene H. Peterson. © 1993, 1994, 1995, 1996, 2000. Used by permission of NavPress Publishing Group. All rights reserved.

Scripture quotations marked GW are taken from GOD'S WORD Translation. Copyright © 1995 by God's Word to the Nations. Used by permission of Baker Publishing Group.

**Library of Congress Cataloging-in-Publication Data**

Parrish, Kristen.
  No cape required : 52 ways to unleash your inner hero / Kristen Parrish.
    pages cm.
  Includes bibliographical references.
  Summary: "What do Katniss Everdeen, Spider-Man, and Huckleberry Finn have in common? They're heroes;and you can be just like them. As children, we dream of throwing on a cape and changing the world. Then we grow up, we learn to see the flaws in our movie stars and athletes, and we accept that true heroism is not possible in the real world. You continue to dream, though. Isn't that why you still love watching heroes on the big screen? It's more than just wish fulfillment. You resonate with Superman's justice and Dorothy's courage because you have those same qualities within yourself. In these pages, Kristen Parrish looks at the qualities of fifty-two heroes, and then shows how you can acquire every one of those qualities. No gamma rays or radioactive spider bites are needed. You can unleash your inner hero through prayer and practical action. Men and women, boys and girls alike, will find role models within these pages. While others watch and dream on the sidelines, you can step out in faith, learning from heroic examples and praying for God's help to make you who you were meant to be. The Holy Spirit enables us to do great things. Find out how. No cape required. —provided by publisher.
  ISBN 978-1-4002-0515-8 (pbk.)
  1. Christianity and the arts. 2. Devotional literature. 3. Christian life. I. Parrish, Kristen. II. Title.
  BR115.A8P365 2013
  248.4—dc23                                                                                    2013014436

*Printed in the United States of America*

13 14 15 16 17 18 RRD 6 5 4 3 2 1

To Sarah, who has grown into
a lovely young woman.

*For he has rescued us from the dominion of darkness*
*and brought us into the kingdom of the Son he loves.*

**—Colossians 1:13** <small>NIV</small>

*We won't begin to understand our lives, or what*
*this so-called gospel is that Christianity speaks*
*of, until we understand the Story in which we*
*have found ourselves. For when you were born,*
*you were born into an Epic that has already been*
*under way for quite some time. It is a story of*
*beauty and intimacy and adventure, a Story of*
*danger and loss and heroism and betrayal.*

**—John Eldredge,** *Epic*

# Contents

# Foreword

by Jefferson Bethke

There is this real peculiar moment toward the end of Jesus' public ministry where he is talking to the gatekeepers of his day and he quotes a Hebrew psalm by saying, "Have you never read in the Scriptures: 'The stone the builders rejected has become the cornerstone; the Lord has done this, and it is marvelous in our eyes'" (Matthew 21:42). I've always been one to pick up on extreme awkwardness in situations (it takes someone being awkward to have this Spidey sense for awkwardness per se) but it doesn't take an expert to see how palpable it is here.

Jesus is talking to the most versed, learned, and religious people of his day and he says, *"Have you never read the Scriptures?"* It's like me saying to Lebron James, *"Have you ever played basketball?"* But what Jesus was getting at was they might have been extremely studied in the Old Testament and its prophecies about this messiah figure God had promised—but they couldn't even see the King himself living, breathing, and talking right in front of them.

But to some degree you can't blame them. Everyone in their particular context was looking for an earthly political or military rebel leader to rise up and take down the pagan empire of Rome and establish God's reign and rule. They expected a *hero. What they got did not meet their expectations.* He didn't look the part. He didn't do what they thought a messiah should. He had no form or majesty in him that would've drawn out anyone's attention. They wanted Superman, but it looked like they got Clark Kent instead.

In that last sentence, though, lies the beauty and mystery of this Jesus from Nazareth. The beauty of Clark Kent is that he is Superman. And while people might have called Clark names and thought he really didn't do much, he was also the one truly saving the day and bringing salvation to Metropolis even though he didn't get the credit as Clark.

In fact, most people thought Jesus lost at the Cross, but looking back we see that was the moment of his ultimate victory. In that dark, violent, crushing event he exhausted the powers of evil, brought them on himself so that his people didn't have to. He saved the day, not how people wanted, but he did save the day. And he invites us into this peculiar way. This upside-down kingdom. This mentality where there is no cape required.

Kristen has written a beautiful, extremely practical devotional that I know will bless you all emphatically. The truths in the beginning of each section are profound and anyone and everyone can do the practical calls-to-action at the end of each chapter. These themes that draw us so deeply into the stories of our classic heroes—Superman, Spider-Man, Wonder Woman—are only shadows. Shadows of the Great Narrative where God himself saw his people in distress, and went to great lengths, even death itself, to rescue us. The heroes in this book aren't destinations, they are signposts. Signposts to our Resurrected King Jesus.

And because of this King's victory, he has given us his Spirit. The Spirit that resurrected him from the clutches of death is also in us. A Spirit that doesn't require capes for admission, but instead brokenness and need serve as our badges. This book will change you.

Kristen has drawn out our love for these fictional characters and pointed us to the man named Truth. And he makes it emphatically clear if you are going to follow him, there's no cape required.

# Introduction

It was an ugly summer. On TV I watched the presidential candidates take turns slinging mud at each other until I didn't really want to vote for either of them. Death counts continued to rise among soldiers based in Afghanistan. And the economy was stuck in the doldrums. Not exactly the kind of environment to put a smile on my face.

Then came *The Avengers*. It became the first movie to cross the $100 million mark in its second weekend while also crossing the $1 billion worldwide total mark. Its North American release gave it the biggest film opening of all time, beating movies such as *Harry Potter and the Deathly Hallows* and *The Dark Knight*.

When families all over the globe were watching every penny, how is it possible they spent so much money on a movie? The answer isn't all that hard, actually. We're in search of heroes, and we'll take them where we can find them. When real heroes are in short supply, we turn to our movies, our books, and our comics to find people we can look up to.

We tire of seeing celebrities falling prey to adultery, politicians lying, athletes using performance enhancers, crime rates rising, and overall politeness going the way of the dinosaurs. We ache for something good and pure, a little taste of what was and of what can still be again. We find it in our fictional heroes: the protectiveness of Katniss Everdeen from *The Hunger Games*, the wisdom of Yoda from *Star Wars*, the courage of Jo March from *Little Women*, the devotion of Samwise Gamgee from *The Lord of the Rings*. And as we identify with their tales, it will become clear that we, too, are called to be heroes in our own right.

Scripture is replete with admonitions to each of us to incorporate heroic characteristics into our own lives. We are to judge righteously (Prov. 31:9), look to the interests of others (Phil. 2:4), have the same mind-set as Christ (Phil. 2:5), be truthful (Eph. 6:14), and walk uprightly (Ps. 84:11).

The good news is that being a hero requires no cape. No matter our age or position, we each have the Holy Spirit to enable us to do great things. And we have innumerable models, examples, and inspirations. I have fifty-two of them in this book. A few of the examples wear capes, but whether it's Superman, Mr. Spock, or Indiana Jones, each tells us something unique and useful about how to be the hero God wants every one of us to be. Since there's one for each week of the year, you can read straight through or use the book as a devotional, taking the week to pray about and apply the specific characteristic mentioned in the chapter. I have offered some suggested action steps with each chapter to help get you started.

I've chosen each character based on one of his or her exemplary traits, but this is not to say they're perfect individuals. Like each of us, they are flawed people living less-than-perfect lives. In fact, some of them are downright ornery or have personality traits that make them folks you'd rather avoid. But also like each of us, there's something redemptive to be found in each one, a special trait that makes that individual capable of much more than he or she would normally be. With God's help, you'll discover that the ability to be a hero is within you too—and has been all along.

# 1
# Justice

*The way of the just is uprightness.*

—Isaiah 26:7

It was not America's finest hour. The year was 1938; the nation was still stuck in the economic malaise following the Great Depression. Putting food on the table was tops on our minds, and those with decent jobs were among the lucky ones. Organized crime was in its heyday—justice was in short supply. To make matters even more ominous, another world war was hovering at the door and threatening to involve the nation again.

Into this depressing environment stepped—or was it flew?—a hero, someone who struck the chords of patriotism and ignited something in our hearts. Two men, artist Joe Shuster and writer Jerry Siegel, gave America Superman, a red, white, and blue crime fighter, right when we needed him most.

From that time through today, DC Comics' Superman has reigned supreme among our most beloved superheroes. His motto: "Truth, justice and the American way." It is the second of these honorable objectives that we saw our superhero pursue most actively in 1978's *Superman: The Movie.* After uttering these iconic words to Lois Lane during an interview, Superman busied himself rendering justice as he turned over to police a cat burglar escaping with jewelry, halted mobsters running away in a boat with their loot after a shootout, and thwarted the evil Lex Luthor's plot to annihilate California.

> Two men gave America Superman, a red, white, and blue crime fighter, right when we needed him most.

Our world today is actually very similar to that of 1938, with crime and poverty rampant, and we're no less in need of a hero to bring justice. Without a Superman in sight, though, it falls on each of us to bring justice to our little corner of the world. God says His way is uprightness (Isa. 26:7), and He is counting on us to do our part. As Christians we are to do justice, love mercy, and walk humbly with our God (Mic. 6:8). God laid it out so simply for us. It's certainly not hard to find people who could use our help. Defend the defenseless; help the oppressed; speak up for the weak! It's our job.

## A PRAYER

Lord, I may not be wealthy or powerful, but in Your will I, too, can work wonders. Please show me where I can bring justice to the people around me or provide support to those who do. Amen.

## TAKE ACTION

- Log on to the website of the Fraternal Order of Police (www.fop.net) or your local police department's website and see what charities they are working with that you may want to support.
- Make cookies for someone involved in civilian public safety—cops on the beat or 911 operators—just to let them know you appreciate what they do. If you have children, have them include a note or picture as appropriate for their age.
- Get involved with the Neighborhood Watch group in your neighborhood or subdivision.

# 2
# Friendship

Mr. Spock and Captain Kirk, *Star Trek*

> *Greater love has no one than this, than*
> *to lay down one's life for his friends.*
> —John 15:13

What's the most famous friendship in the history of pop culture? My money is on Captain James T. Kirk and his Vulcan first officer, Mr. Spock, from Gene Roddenberry's *Star Trek*. Where the rugged captain played from his gut, often finding unique solutions to dangerous encounters, Spock was his ever-logical and supremely faithful counterpart. Whether they were facing Romulans or Klingons or nemeses like Khan Noonien Singh, together they made a whole. And their relationship has endured since the original television show premiered in 1966.

It is no small thing when in 1982's movie, *Star Trek II: The Wrath of Khan*, Mr. Spock faces his final moments separated from his friend by a clear wall. How does he end up

William Shatner and Leonard Nimoy as Admiral James T. Kirk and Captain Spock in *Star Trek II: The Wrath Of Khan*, directed by Nicholas Meyer

stranded and alone? The wounded *Enterprise* is desperately trying to escape an exploding nebula, but without warp speed, they'll never make it. Spock quietly disappears from the bridge and descends to the engine room, where he restores the warp drive, knowing the leaking radiation will be fatal to him.

"I have been, and always shall be, your friend."

—SPOCK, TO ADMIRAL KIRK

With the ship out of danger, now-Admiral Kirk rushes down to his friend but cannot even hold him as he dies, because of the radiation that has flooded the engine room.

"Spock!" Kirk cries.

"The ship . . . out of danger?" asks his friend.

"Yes."

"Don't grieve, Admiral," Spock says weakly. "It is logical. The needs of the many outweigh—"

"—the needs of the few," supplies Kirk.

"Or the one . . . I have been, and always shall be, your friend." Spock holds up his hand in the iconic Vulcan salute. "Live long and prosper."

Spock's dying statements to his friend mirror those found in Scripture. It is essentially the same message Jesus gave us in John 15:12–13, where He commanded us to love one another "as I have loved you. Greater love has no one than this, than to lay down one's life for his friends."

Friendship is a gift that God gives to us, just as He gave

it to David and Jonathan in 1 Samuel 18:1: "And it came to pass, when he had made an end of speaking unto Saul, that the soul of Jonathan was knit with the soul of David, and Jonathan loved him as his own soul" (KJV). These men were friends to the end, and after Jonathan was killed in battle, David took his friend's son into his household to raise as his own child.

Is your life rich with friendships? If you are one of the luckiest of us, you may have a friend whom you love as your own soul. Be sure to nurture that relationship and consider yourself a blessed person.

## A PRAYER

Dear Lord, thank You for friends. Help me appreciate them and not take them for granted. Show me who to offer my friendship. Amen.

## TAKE ACTION

- Is there someone new in your community? Reach out the hand of friendship and welcome her or him.
- Do you have old friendships you've allowed to wither away for lack of time? Reenergize them with a quick phone call, a Facebook message, or an e-mail, letting them know you're thinking about them.

- Is there someone in your church or elsewhere in your daily life who doesn't have many friends because he or she is socially awkward or shy? Offer your friendship, and you may be surprised what a delight you are to that person.

# 3
# Hope in Others

Belle, *Beauty and the Beast*

> *Let us hold fast the confession of our hope without*
> *wavering, for He who promised is faithful. And*
> *let us consider one another in order to stir up love*
> *and good works, not forsaking the assembling*
> *of ourselves together, as is the manner of some,*
> *but exhorting one another, and so much the*
> *more as you see the Day approaching.*
>
> —Hebrews 10:23–25

"I'm about ready to give up on this hunk of junk!" hollers Belle's father, kicking the mechanical invention he'd been working on.

"You always say that," replies Belle.

"I mean it, this time. I'll never get this boneheaded contraption to work."

"Yes, you will," she soothes. "And you'll win first prize at the fair tomorrow . . . and become a world-famous inventor!"

"You really believe that?"

"I always have."

As we see in Disney's *Beauty and the Beast*, the beautiful and bookish Belle never gives up hope in those she loves. It's the theme on which her whole story turns, but, just like her father, she faces a situation in which it would have been easier to give up. Instead, she pushes through the difficulty and finds a way to hope in the most unlikely person of all.

Belle is imprisoned in the Beast's castle, held hostage for her father's freedom. Years before, a dark spell had been cast which transformed the prince into a monster and the castle into a dark and scary hold. Only true love can break the spell, and it doesn't look very likely that love will sprout between the young woman and the disagreeable Beast.

> "There's something sweet about him," Belle muses, wondering why she hadn't seen it in him before.

She determines to escape from the castle into the forest. Though daring, the move is foolish. As wolves close in for an attack, who rescues Belle at the risk of his own life? The Beast!

As the Beast's heart opens to Belle, he wants to give her something that would reach hers. He offers his library to her—a huge, wonderful room full to the ceiling with all the books she could dream of.

"There's something sweet about him," Belle muses in

one song, wondering why she hadn't seen it in him before. It is a spark. She is beginning to hope in the Beast.

When the two discover her father is sick and alone, lost and looking for Belle, the Beast loves her enough to set her free to find her father. That's when she discovers that the townspeople, led by the evil Gaston, are setting out to kill the Beast.

"I know he looks vicious," she tries to assure them, "but he's really kind and gentle. He's my friend."

Urged on by Gaston, they ignore Belle and rush to the castle, where Gaston attacks the Beast and stabs him.

"No, no!" cries Belle as she finds the wounded and dying Beast. "Please! Please! Please don't leave me! I love you!"

Those are literally the magic words. The spell is broken, turning the Beast into a handsome prince, restoring the dark castle to its former bright, lustrous beauty—all because Belle wouldn't give up her hard-won hope in the Beast.

Like Belle, you have the power to turn darkness to light. In fact, it only takes the same words Belle used: "I love you." Loving someone breeds hope not only in your heart but in the other person's heart as well. And having love and consideration for others is something we are called to do. As we are loved by our heavenly Savior, Hebrews 10:24 tells us to "consider one another in order to stir up love and good works."

As you go about your day, consider in whom you might stir up hope and love with a few magic words of your own.

## A PRAYER

Dear Jesus, You have told us to love one another. Please show me if there's someone in my life who especially needs to see my love and hope today. Let me help stir up hope in his or her heart. Amen.

## TAKE ACTION

- Someone in your life needs you to have hope for him or her. Pray for that person and let him know your heart is full of hope for him and for what's going on in his life.
- Write notes of encouragement for those closest to you when they're going through tough times. Let them know you have hope for their situation and their future.

# 4

# Mentoring

Mr. Miyagi, *The Karate Kid*

> *My son, pay attention to my wisdom;*
> *Lend your ear to my understanding,*
> *That you may preserve discretion,*
> *And your lips may keep knowledge.*

—Proverbs 5:1–2

Daniel LaRusso is having the worst week of his life. Newly arrived in California from New Jersey, the teenager finds himself experiencing the wrath of Johnny, a malicious young man who has a black belt and a bad attitude. At the beach Daniel meets an attractive young woman named Ali who recently dumped Johnny, and Johnny doesn't appreciate this newcomer infringing on "his" territory. Daniel is repeatedly roughed up by Johnny and his gang, all black belts at a local karate school.

But what is a skinny kid from Jersey to do? He needs help, and he finds it in the unlikely person of Mr. Miyagi, an old man who is the groundskeeper for the apartment complex where Daniel and his mother live. Originally from Okinawa, Mr. Miyagi learned karate from his father, and he reluctantly agrees to take on Daniel as a pupil. He is concerned, however, that Daniel's main reason for wanting to learn karate is revenge. "You look for revenge that way, start by digging two graves," says Mr. Miyagi in accented English. "Fighting always last answer to problem."

> "You look for revenge that way, start by digging two graves. Fighting always last answer to problem."
>
> —MR. MIYOGI TO DANIEL

Nevertheless, the training begins, but not in the way Daniel expected. First Mr. Miyagi has Daniel wax his antique car collection. "Wax on, right hand. Wax off, left hand. Wax on, wax off." The next lesson, he has him sand his wooden floor. "Right circle, left circle. Breathe in, breathe out." Finally he has him paint his fence: "All in wrist. Wrist up. Wrist down." All of this frustrates Daniel to no end, but he is astounded when he realizes Mr. Miyagi has been training him all along in the basic moves of karate.

Mr. Miyagi finds an honorable way for Daniel to fight Johnny—at a karate tournament. And despite the fact that Johnny fights dirty and injures Daniel's leg, Daniel wins, using a midair kicking jump, Mr. Miyagi's "Crane" technique.

Many of us have had a Mr. Miyagi in our lives, and although we may not have faced off against someone in a karate tournament, our direction has been completely transformed by someone who took the time to invest in us. If you are a teenager or an adult, you have the opportunity to be someone's Mr. Miyagi. Have you ever considered mentoring a student at a local school? This one-on-one time can be as short as an hour a week and yet make an indelible impression on a youngster. Or perhaps you're called to something that takes a bigger commitment, like a Big Brother or Big Sister program. If you feel this tug toward mentoring, it may be God's way of saying, "Wax on, wax off," and preparing your heart for something new.

## A PRAYER

Dear Father, if You would have me mentor someone, please speak clearly to my heart and direct me in the path You would have me go. Amen.

## TAKE ACTION

- Pray about becoming a mentor and see if God is pointing you in this direction.
- Start right where you are. You can take a more intentional mentoring role right in your home with your own kids or younger siblings, or maybe someone from church or school.

- If you think mentoring is for you, call a local school or the Boys & Girls Club and see if they have a mentoring program suited to your skills that you could take part in.

# 5
# Charity

Robin Hood

*Open your mouth, judge righteously,*
*And plead the cause of the poor and needy.*

—Proverbs 31:9

His name is Robin Hood, and he's been around in ballads and tales since medieval times. The lines below, from about the year 1450, written in Middle English, are from one of the oldest ballads about the "courteous outlaw":

> *LYTHE and listin, gentilmen,*
> *That be of frebore blode;*
> *I shall you tel of a gode yeman,*
> *His name was Robyn Hode.*
>
> *Robyn was a prude outlaw,*
> *[Whyles he walked on grounde;*
> *So curteyse an outlawe] as he was one*
> *Was never non founde.*

Frederick Warde as Robin Hood, illustration by Wm. Greer Harrison, created and copyright 1895 by the Strobridge Lith Co., Cinti, NY.

In more modern times, Robin Hood graced the silver screen in a 1908 black-and-white silent film called *Robin Hood and His Merry Men*. Since then he has been played by Douglas Fairbanks, Errol Flynn, Sean Connery, Kevin Costner, and Russell Crowe. In a Disney adaptation, an animated fox played the wily bandit.

The allure of Robin Hood over the centuries is simple to understand: our hearts respond to a man who devotes his life to opposing the unjust and helping the poor. Tales of Robin Hood are rife with examples of his charity toward those in need. In Scripture we read that Jesus' heart is also for the poor among us. In Matthew 25:37–40, He makes it clear:

> Then the righteous will answer Him, saying, "Lord, when did we see You hungry and feed You, or thirsty and give You drink? When did we see You a stranger and take You in, or naked and clothe You? Or when did we see You sick, or in prison, and come to You?" And the King will answer and say to them, "Assuredly, I say to you, inasmuch as you did it to one of the least of these My brethren, you did it to Me."

Are you one of the generous souls who ministers to the hungry, the sick, the imprisoned? If so, Christ says you have ministered to Him. And next time you see Robin Hood in a movie or on TV, remember that, like the "courteous out-law," you are giving back to "the least of these."

## A PRAYER

Heavenly Father, I am so grateful to You for the opportunities You've given me to help people in need. I know that by doing so I'm in the center of Your will. Help me to recognize You in the eyes of strangers who need me and to respond to them in love. Amen.

## TAKE ACTION

- Bring flowers to a retirement home and give them to someone who never has visitors.
- Clean out your closets and donate your gently used clothing to a charity that clothes the down-and-out.
- Contact a ministry that serves prisoners or homeless veterans and ask if there's something you can do to help.

# 6
# Hope

Andy Dufresne, *The Shawshank Redemption*

*He shall call upon Me, and I will answer him;*
*I will be with him in trouble;*
*I will deliver him and honor him.*

—Psalm 91:15

Andy Dufresne had every reason to despair. Wrongly convicted of the murder of his wife and her golf-pro lover, he faces two lifetime sentences in Shawshank prison. It is a brutal existence, where he endures beatings, and worse, from fellow inmates, and where the guards are more evil than most of the prisoners.

As the years pass, Andy manages to gain the trust of the warden and is allowed to take over the pathetic little prison library. One day, along with boxes of donated books, he receives a recording of Italian opera. The ever-so-well-behaved Andy suddenly decides to lock his guard in the bathroom, turn on the prison-wide speaker system, and crank up the beautiful music—to the amazement and delight of the prisoners. Andy pays for his prank with time in solitary confinement.

After he emerges from the dark hellhole, he eats breakfast with his friend Red. Andy tells Red, "[It was the] easiest time I ever did . . . I had Mr. Mozart to keep me company. Hardly felt the time at all . . . Here's where it makes most sense. We need it so we don't forget."

Red asks, "Forget?"

"That there are things in this world not carved out of gray stone. That there's a small place inside of us they can never lock away, and that place is called hope."

It turns out Andy never did give up on hope. To everyone's amazement he escapes prison by using a tiny pickax, removing rock for almost twenty years until he tunnels out to a sewer pipe that empties outside the prison. Red, too, ends up on the outside after he is paroled, and finds that Andy has left a letter for him: "Remember, Red. Hope is a good thing, maybe the best of things, and no good thing ever dies. I will be hoping that this letter finds you, and finds you well. Your friend, Andy." The two friends end up together on a beach in Mexico—the vision Andy had painted for Red in Shawshank.

Do you find yourself without hope at times? Has a close friend turned his or her back on you? Is your family falling apart? Is everything going wrong at school? Is your marriage or relationship at a breaking point? Your job draining? Your spiritual life in the doldrums? Perhaps an illness plagues you, or your children are misbehaving. Life itself can weigh heavy.

We face so many obstacles in life that it can certainly lead us to despair. Even David, who had seen Goliath fall to a stone from his slingshot and had seen God deliver the Israelites in battle, had his moments where all seemed hopeless. Because he was an Israelite, he would have known about God's faithfulness in Scripture from the time he was a little boy, yet he still had times where life seemed dim. But remember that, like David, we have Someone to turn to who will not fail us. God promises that if we call on Him, He will not fail; He will deliver us.

> "[It was the] easiest time I ever did . . . I had Mr. Mozart to keep me company."
>
> **—ANDY DUFRESNE TO RED**

Keep in mind the situation you are in may not resolve the way you expect. Perhaps the answer to your prayer is something you never anticipated or didn't think possible, like a change in your perspective toward your situation. Hold to God's promises and His love, and He will be with you in your time of trouble.

## A PRAYER

Dear God, sometimes my life seems so full of troubles I can't see how it can ever be made right.

In those times, please help me remember that You promise to be with me in times of trouble. You hold me in Your arms with love. Amen.

## TAKE ACTION

- Have you ever prayed unceasingly for something? Choose one thing in your life—or in someone else's—that needs a solution, and saturate it with prayer this week.
- Assemble a "hope kit" for someone at a homeless shelter and drop it off. Fill it with the necessities and include a note of hope.

# 7

# Repentance

Eustace Scrubb, *The Chronicles of Narnia*

> *In him we have redemption through his blood,*
> *the forgiveness of sins, in accordance with*
> *the riches of God's grace that he lavished on*
> *us with all wisdom and understanding.*

—**Ephesians 1:7–8** NIV

Eustace Clarence Scrubb is not a nice boy. In fact, his cousin Edmund says he deserves his name, and it is true. He is selfish and particularly detests Edmund and his sister Lucy. Eustace wrote in his journal,

> Dear Diary, it is now day 253 since my wretched cousins Edmund and Lucy invaded our house. Not sure how much longer I can cope living with them, having to share my things. If only one could treat relatives like one treats insects, all my problems would be solved. I could simply put them in a jar, or pin them to a wall

[like an insect]. Note to self: investigate legal implications of impaling relatives.

When he is transported with Edmund and Lucy to Narnia, it's no surprise that he is extremely unpleasant. "I demand to know just where in the blazes am I?" he declares.

Despite his protestations, the adventures begin, and he is drawn along, finding new ways to be unhelpful and cowardly. When the rest of the crew are fighting a battle on an island, Eustace creeps away alone to try to escape instead of helping seal the victory. And when he is supposed to be the lookout, he allows himself to be captured by the enemy, putting the rest of the crew in danger.

> "If only one could treat relatives like one treats insects, all my problems would be solved."
>
> **—EUSTACE SCRUBB**

Finally, through his greed, he succumbs to a spell that turns him into a dragon. It is only now, after the situation has become impossibly dire, that he begins to repent of his bad behavior and dedicate himself to changing. When a giant sea monster attacks the ship, it is Eustace the dragon who fights it off, getting injured in the process. And again he comes to the rescue when the ship is caught in the doldrums; he pulls it along with his tail until it is able to find the wind again. No matter what he does, however, he is still trapped under the spell, doomed to live as a dragon for the rest of his life. It isn't until Aslan steps into the picture with his miraculous powers that Eustace is able to become a boy again.

Eustace's predicament is more similar to yours than you may think. Like him, we live trapped in our sin, unable to find an escape by our own means. Even though we may recognize it and become repentant about our behavior, we still require something from God. It's a thing called grace, and we can't earn it; we can only receive it.

To get to that point, we must humble ourselves and ask for grace. "Let us then approach God's throne of grace with confidence, so that we may receive mercy and find grace to help us in our time of need" (Heb. 4:16 NIV).

Do you have sin in your life that is suffocating you? It's time to lay it down before the throne of Christ and ask for grace. He gives it abundantly!

## A PRAYER

Dear God, some days I feel like Eustace Scrubb, trapped in my sin. Thank You for the grace You offer so that I may live without that terrible weight. Amen.

## TAKE ACTION

- List three sins you repent of, and pray for forgiveness and grace for them.

- The next time someone does something that makes you angry, try giving a little grace yourself. (This is particularly helpful in traffic!)

# 8

# Quiet Service

Alfred Pennyworth, Loyal Manservant to Batman

*For even the Son of Man came not to be served but
to serve, and to give his life as a ransom for many.*

—**Mark 10:45** ESV

Depending on your age, you may have eagerly handed over your change to the drugstore clerk to buy the latest *Batman* comic book. Or maybe you rushed home from school to catch the next cliffhanger episode of *Batman and Robin* on TV—"same bat-time, same bat-channel." Perhaps you're a little younger than that, and your main interaction with the Caped Crusader has been through the Warner Bros. animated series or the many *Batman* movies. No matter where you've encountered this hero, though, Alfred Pennyworth—Bruce Wayne's loyal and tireless butler, valet, friend, and father figure—has been a constant.

While Batman is out mixing it up with dastardly enemies, he knows with utter certainty that back at Wayne Manor resides someone who's taking care of everything else, someone he can trust to keep all his secrets, who cares about him as much as any father, and who—through his quiet service—makes it possible for Batman to do what he does.

Resourceful and unflappable, Alfred may not be the one having the exciting adventures, but he is a vital part of Wayne's life, with skills as varied as maintaining the batmobile, building the batcomputer, and keeping the Caped Crusader's costume in pristine condition. Alfred also provides his employer first aid, including removing bullets, so Batman doesn't have to go to the hospital when he's injured.

Depending on which comic book series you follow, the suave manservant has also mastered "rose breeding (even creating his own, the 'Pennyworth Blue'), computer programming, computer engineering, electrical engineering, chemical engineering, mechanical engineering, nanotechnology, and biotechnology, as he singlehandedly builds programs and maintains much of Batman's next-generational technology."

But you don't have to maintain a batmobile or program a batcomputer to be an Alfred. You are an Alfred if you provide quiet service, tending the home fires and taking care of others so that when they're out in the cold, cruel world, they know someone is at home who knows all their secrets, loves them anyway, and makes it possible for them to do what they do.

In our culture, being a servant is often considered a lowly occupation, and we try to avoid the types of jobs servanthood entails. But Jesus talked about service often, and He modeled it for us as well, doing things such as washing His disciples' feet. After performing this task, Jesus said, "I have given you an example to follow. Do as I have done to you" (John 13:14–15 NLT). It doesn't get much clearer than that: We are to serve others. In this way we are actually serving God.

> You don't have to maintain a batmobile or program a batcomputer to be an Alfred.

## A PRAYER

Dear Lord, thank You for the Alfreds You have placed in my life, and thank You for the opportunities You've given me to be someone else's Alfred. Please help me recognize that quiet service is just as valuable— if not even more so—than the more obvious acts of service can be. Amen.

## TAKE ACTION

- Identify someone who has no Alfred in his or her life, and perform an act of quiet service for that person.

- Call someone who has been an Alfred to you, and thank him or her.
- Be an Alfred to your significant other, a close friend, your parent, or a child, and make that loved one's favorite meal tonight, just because.

# 9

# Kindness

Melanie, *Gone with the Wind*

> *Return to the LORD your God,*
> *For He is gracious and merciful,*
> *Slow to anger, and of great kindness.*

> —Joel 2:13

Kindness is certainly not one of Scarlett O'Hara's virtues. Selfish and vain, the lovely young heroine of *Gone with the Wind* is in love with George Ashley Wilkes, and she doesn't have charitable feelings toward Melanie Hamilton, who, rumor has it, will soon receive a marriage proposal from him. "Melanie Hamilton," Scarlett complains to her father, "she's a pale-faced, mealy-mouthed ninny, and I hate her . . . Ashley Wilkes couldn't like anyone like her." But Melanie is the antithesis of Scarlett, without a mean bone in her body. At Wilkes's party the next day, Scarlett flirts with all the adoring young men who attend. Later she overhears other women who are gossiping about her, one

Olivia de Havilland as Melanie Wilkes in *Gone with the Wind*, directed by
Victor Fleming and George Cukor (MGM, 1939).

of them saying, "Well, she certainly made a fool of herself running after all the men at the barbeque."

It is Melanie who comes to her defense. "That's not fair, India. She's just so attractive the men just naturally flock to her. . . . Scarlett's just high-spirited and vivacious."

"Well, men may flirt with women like that, but they don't marry them," the woman says cruelly.

"I think you're being very mean to her," Melanie gently reprimands her. It isn't the last time Scarlett is the object of Melanie's unwarranted kindness. Despite the fact that Scarlett is in love with Melanie's husband, Melanie repeatedly comes to her defense.

After the war is over, Scarlett tries to manipulate Wilkes into coming to Atlanta and helping to run her lumber mill—anything to keep the man close to her. Faking it, she begins to cry.

"Ashley's so mean and hateful," she cries to Melanie, who came when she heard Scarlett's sobs.

"She wanted me to go to Atlanta," Wilkes tries to explain.

"—to help me start my lumber business. He won't lift a finger to help me," Scarlett continues.

"How unchivalrous of you," Melanie says to her husband, listing the ways Scarlett has helped her. "Why, think, Ashley, think. If it hadn't been for Scarlett, I'd have died in Atlanta. And maybe we wouldn't have had little Beau. And when I think of her picking cotton and plowing just to keep food in our mouths—oh, my darling," she says as she hugs Scarlett.

Wilkes finally gives in to the inevitable. "All right Melanie, I'll go to Atlanta. I can't fight you both."

In Atlanta Melanie comes to Scarlett's defense yet again. The town gossips witness Scarlett and Wilkes caught in an embrace. Everyone soon knows, and nothing can save Scarlett's reputation . . . except Melanie, who welcomes Scarlett into her home for her husband's birthday party and stands with her in front of the townspeople, calling her "our darling Scarlett" and refusing to believe the gossip she's heard about her beloved friend.

"How does it feel to have the woman you've wronged cloak your sins for you?" later demands Scarlett's husband, Rhett Butler. "You're wondering if she knows all about you and Ashley. You're wondering if she did it just to save her face. You're thinking that she's a fool for doing it even if it did save your hide . . . Miss Melanie's a fool, but not the kind you think. It's just that's there's too much honor in her to ever conceive of dishonor in anyone she loves. And she loves you. Though just why she does, I'm sure I don't know."

> "How does it feel to have the woman you've wronged cloak your sins for you?"
>
> **—RHETT BUTLER, TO SCARLETT**

Melanie's kindness lasts to the very end of her life. As Melanie is dying, she asks for Scarlett. "Look after my little son," she says to her. "Ashley and you . . . look after him for me just as you looked after me for him."

Rhett says of Melanie after her death: "She was the only completely kind person I ever knew." Melanie had that special kindness that comes from giving grace. It's undeserved and priceless, like the kindness the Lord shows for us every day. Despite the fact that we continually fall short, He loves us and desires the best for us.

In the book of Joel, God calls for the Israelites to repent and come back to Him, wanting so badly to be kind to them:

> *"Now, therefore," says the Lord,*
> *"Turn to Me with all your heart,*
> *With fasting, with weeping, and with mourning."*
> *So rend your heart, and not your garments;*
> *Return to the Lord your God,*
> *For He is gracious and merciful,*
> *Slow to anger, and of great kindness;*
> *And He relents from doing harm. (2:12–13)*

Our culture is abysmally short on kindness, and it's easier to find the Scarlett-type behavior than Melanie's. Check out any of the reality TV shows for confirmation of that. Let us instead follow the example of our God and resolve to be the example of kindness He desires for us.

## A PRAYER

Lord God, it's more natural for me to have Scarlett's selfish tendencies than Melanie's quality of kindness. Please help me recognize that in myself and to choose kindness whenever possible. Amen.

## TAKE ACTION

- Resolve that the next time you hear gossip, you'll not take part in it.
- List three ways you can show kindness to others, and follow through with them this week.
- Memorize Galatians 5:22–26, which lists the fruit of the spirit, including kindness.

# 10

# Tender Care

U.S. Marshal Reuben J. "Rooster"
Cogburn, *True Grit*

*Let each of you look not only to his own*
*interests, but also to the interests of others.*

—**Philippians 2:4** ESV

When we first meet fourteen-year-old Mattie Ross in *True Grit*, her father has been killed by the family's hired hand, Tom Chaney, while the two men were away on business. Bold and clever, Mattie arrives to settle matters. When she approaches the sheriff about arresting the killer, however, he can do no better than advise her about which U.S. marshal might best earn the bounty she is prepared to put on Chaney's head.

Among the list of names is Rooster Cogburn, whom the sheriff describes as mean, pitiless, double-tough, and fearless. In a word, he has *grit*. Mattie chooses Rooster to apprehend her father's killer, but Rooster will have none of it. Rooster suffers from more than a few character flaws—one of which is being a lazy drunk. But he finally agrees to take on Mattie's case because the job pays a hundred dollars, fifty up front.

Getting Chaney is Mattie's goal, but making sure Mattie comes through safely becomes Cogburn's only real concern. The first hint of this is when Texas Ranger LaBoeuf tries taking a switch to Mattie's behind. Rather than let him whip the girl, Rooster draws his revolver, points it at LaBoeuf, and tells him to stop or he'll regret it.

> Rooster Cogburn has grit, but what really makes him heroic is his heart.

Rooster sticks with Mattie through one thing after another, until finally, Chaney, now running with the infamous Ned Pepper Gang, captures the girl. Rooster agrees with Pepper to leave the girl behind in exchange for her life. But having rejoined LaBoeuf, Rooster sends him to free Mattie while he faces down Ned Pepper.

In the ensuing fight, Mattie kills Chaney but falls down a mine shaft and is bitten by a rattler. The image is Christlike: Rooster descends into the pit, kills the snake, and pulls out the wounded Mattie. His only concern is getting her to safety. Rooster hauls Mattie and places her on the saddle of her pony and drives the horse through the late afternoon, through the evening, into the night, finally riding the poor animal into the ground, trying to get Mattie to medical attention. After the horse collapses, Rooster scoops the girl up into his arms and starts running. The Coen Brothers' film adaptation makes the gospel connection clear. "Leaning on the Everlasting Arms" plays as Rooster carries Mattie to safety.

Somewhere along the way, Rooster takes to calling Mattie "little sister." After reaching help, he stays with her until his little sister is out of all danger. The picture is clear: Rooster Cogburn has grit, but what really makes him heroic is his heart. Beneath that mean, pitiless, double-tough exterior, the man cares.

## A PRAYER

Heavenly Father, give me a heart to care for those around me. When I am cold to their plight, give me sympathy. When I am moved, empower me to act. Whatever my attitude or resources, help me use them for the sake of others. Amen.

## TAKE ACTION

- When you see someone—anyone—in need, step out and help. God will bring you people like Mattie who need your heart, if you'll open it enough to see them coming.
- Who could use your care today, this week, this month? Write down a few names and look for ways to serve them.

- Do you have a Facebook friend going through a tough time? Do more than just comment that you'll pray for him or her. Set aside time in your prayer life to devote to that person this week, and follow up with your friend to see how he or she is doing.

# 11
# Protectiveness

Katniss Everdeen, *The Hunger Games*

> "And I will pray the Father, and He
> will give you another Helper."
>
> —John 14:16

Twelve-year-old Primrose is terrified. It seeps into her sleep and wakes her with nightmare images and screams that bring her older sister, Katniss, rushing to her side. "Shhh. It's okay. You were dreaming . . . They're not going to pick you."

Katniss, too, is worried about her sister. Prim is old enough this year to be eligible for the Reaping, the annual choosing of two young people from each district, who will then fight to the death with those from the eleven other districts in a brutal televised competition known as the Hunger Games. How can she protect her from that real nightmare?

The next day, Prim's worst fears come true when it is her name that is pulled from the jar as the "winner." As the little girl slowly makes her way to the front, Katniss breaks from the crowd, shouting, "I volunteer as tribute!" With those words Katniss takes her sister's place, knowing she is quite probably signing her own death warrant.

> As the little girl slowly makes her way to the front, Katniss breaks from the crowd, shouting, "I volunteer as tribute!"

At the games, Katniss does not play by the rules. While the other kids slaughter each other in the woods and fields where the Hunger Games take place, she never goes hunting for the other contestants. And when she meets one of them, a little girl named Rue, her natural instinct is to protect her, and she takes her in. Later, she risks her life to come out of hiding to obtain desperately needed medicine for her friend Peeta. And in the end, she survives.

Like Primrose, Rue, and Peeta, we, too, have a helper and a protector. Jesus told us,

> "If you love Me, keep My commandments. And I will pray the Father, and He will give you another Helper, that He may abide with you forever—the Spirit of truth, whom the world cannot receive, because it neither sees Him nor knows Him; but you know Him, for He dwells with you and will be in you. I will not leave you orphans; I will come to you." (John 14:15–18)

The Holy Spirit already dwells in each believer, assuring us that we will never face alone what life throws at us. God also promises us that He'll be our strong tower. Proverbs 18:10 says, "The name of the LORD is a strong tower; the righteous run to it and are safe." That means when your own strength fails, you can depend on His.

Next time you're feeling as scared and vulnerable as Prim, remember you already have a hero who dwells in you and a strong tower to escape to. Wrap yourself in that knowledge, and you'll be the braver for it. Perhaps you can even be strong for someone else.

## A PRAYER

Dear Jesus, there are people all around me who need protection in some way. Please help me know who they are, and guide me in providing them what they may need. Amen.

## TAKE ACTION

- List people in your life who need prayer for their protection. It may be a friend who is struggling with peer pressure or bullying or who is experiencing abuse from a spouse or a dating partner. This week concentrate your prayers on those people and their needs.

- Find an organization that supports women coming out of abusive situations and offer to help by providing material support or a little bit of your time.

# 12

# Growth

Robin / Dick Grayson, *Batman Forever*

*Hold fast the pattern of sound words*
*which you have heard from me, in faith*
*and love which are in Christ Jesus.*

—2 Timothy 1:13

We all remember our younger years with a little bit of a cringe, don't we? "Why did I say that?" "What on earth was I thinking?" "Why didn't I listen to my mother?" Turns out there was a good explanation for some of our seemingly inane decisions—our brains truly were not finished developing, and in fact this process continues into young adulthood. Discovery Fit & Health says that the various parts of the teenage brain don't yet have full capability to work together to make good decisions: "For comparison's sake, think of the teenage brain as an entertainment center that hasn't been fully hooked up. There are loose wires, so that the speaker system isn't working with the DVD player, which in turn hasn't been formatted to work with the television yet. And to top it all off, the remote control hasn't even arrived!"

We can see some of this disarray at work in the mind of young Dick Grayson in *Batman Forever*. When Bruce Wayne takes Grayson in after the murder of Dick's parents by a villain named Two-Face, Grayson is bent on one thing: revenge. "I'm going to get a fix on Two-Face. Then I'm going to kill him," he swears to Wayne.

The older crime fighter has some words of wisdom for Grayson, gleaned from his own experience. "Dick, killing Two-Face won't take the pain away. It'll make it worse."

> "Look, spare me the sermons, okay. You're just some rich guy who is trying to do a good deed. You don't even know me."
>
> **—DICK GRAYSON, TO BRUCE WAYNE**

As with many young people, the good advice doesn't hold much sway with Grayson, and he persists in his goal. "Look, spare me the sermons, okay," he tells Wayne. "You're just some rich guy who is trying to do a good deed. You don't even know me."

Later Grayson discovers—and goes for a joyride in—the batmobile. Now he has a taste for the action, the adventure, that he perceives comes with Bruce's alter ego. Wayne tries to explain that, for him, crime fighting is not about revenge; it is not a game. But Grayson still doesn't have the maturity to understand his point and pushes Wayne away. "Right, slick," Grayson says. "Whatever you say."

We see real growth in Dick Grayson as the movie progresses, and he takes on the persona of Robin. As the dynamic duo faces down Two-Face, Robin finally gets the villain right where he wants him. All that stands between the abyss and Two Face's certain death is Robin, who has him dangling by the hand. Robin hoists him up to safety. "I'd rather see you in jail," he tells Two-Face, who replies, "The Bat's taught you well. Noble."

Robin has grown up.

Hopefully, like Robin, we all keep growing. For the older reader, do you now have a young person in your life whose brain is still waiting for the remote control to arrive? Perhaps knowing that the synapses in his or her brain are still being connected will help give you the same patience Bruce Wayne demonstrated with Dick Grayson.

For the younger reader, remember that God designed us to grow in our faith and our maturity as we age, and be patient with yourself as your remote control finishes its wiring. Although it may not seem like it now, you may be a young superhero in the making yourself.

## A PRAYER

Lord God, thank You for the people in my life who showed me patience during my youth. Give me the wisdom to show younger people grace now that

I'm older. Help me continue to be a mentor rather than give up on them. Amen.

# TAKE ACTION

- Find a younger person doing something right, and comment on it. It may be the only compliment he or she has received in a long time, and it means a lot coming from an older person.
- Call your church's youth group leader or children's director and ask if there's something you can do to help out.

# 13

# Loyalty

Dobby, the *Harry Potter* movies

*A man who has friends must himself be friendly,*
*But there is a friend who sticks closer than a brother.*

—Proverbs 18:24

When most people think about loyalty, their minds either go to Arthurian legends or the family dog—seldom in between. We associate the virtue either with the heroic fighter dedicated to a cause larger than himself, or the furry creature whose devotion seems uncomplicated and instinctual.

Rarely do we think about loyalty as an everyday thing, and we certainly don't associate it with hundreds of young adults dressed up as wizards at bookstores in the middle of the night. However, the small, elfish figure of Dobby, from the *Harry Potter* books and movies, serves as a perfect example of loyalty like that: of personal sacrifice that asks for no recognition at the end of the day.

Though Dobby was born a slave, he repeatedly risks

himself for Harry Potter, saving the boy wizard's life more times than even the most careful reader could count. In the end, Dobby dies saving Harry and his friends from the Dark Lord, laying down his humble life in the process. It's at that point that many *Harry Potter* fans put down our books and mourn for the tiny house elf with a curious and adorable love of knitted socks and neckties; but not many of us thought about what a love like that really is—it's heavenly.

Though Dobby is a beautiful example of loyalty, our little movie hero pales in comparison to the real thing. Proverbs says, "There is a friend who sticks closer than a brother," and indeed, when it came time to sacrifice Himself for us, Christ's loyalty proved supreme. Jesus came to our cold and unloving world to save us from the chain of sin, so heavy it would crush us. Dobby did die to save Harry Potter, but surely if he could have spared himself and still rescued Harry, he would have done that. Every second Jesus was on the cross, He was God, fully capable of saving Himself and punishing those who put Him there. Yet He chose to sacrifice His life for us instead. Moreover, Jesus came back to us. He was perfectly loyal to

> [When Dobby dies,] it's at that point that many *Harry Potter* fans put down our books and mourn for the tiny house elf with a curious and adorable love of knitted socks and neckties.

us in life, in death, and in coming back to life despite our disloyalty to Him. His loyalty is perfect.

Dobby is the kind of friend any of us would love to have, but remember that there's only one person who has already given everything for you. Have you taken the time lately to say thank you to Jesus for His sacrifice?

## A PRAYER

Heavenly Father, thank You for your loyalty to us, especially when we fail to be loyal to You. Please forgive us for that, and help us to remember Your perfect sacrifice on our behalf. Amen.

## TAKE ACTION

- Read 1 Samuel 18–20 to get a taste for the closeness Jonathan and David had. Then read 2 Samuel 9:1–13 to see how loyal David was to his friend after his death.
- Who are you loyal to? Pray for them specifically this week.

# 14

# Truthfulness

Wonder Woman

*Stand therefore, having girded your waist with truth, having put on the breastplate of righteousness.*

—Ephesians 6:14

William Moulton Marston had a strange and winding career path. It included stints as a psychologist, a feminist theorist, an inventor, and a comic-strip writer. During World War I, while looking for a way to identify spies, he created an apparatus to measure systolic blood pressure, which became one of the crucial measurements in the polygraph—"lie detector"—test. Later in his career, Marston hadn't given up on the value of a lie-detecting device, and as a comic-strip writer created

The Magic Lasso of Truth "was unbreakable, infinitely stretchable, and could make all who are encircled in it tell the truth."

not only Wonder Woman but her Golden Lasso of Truth. Because the lasso was, in essence, a lie detector, it extracted the truth from anyone who had the misfortune to find himself trapped in its loop.

Wonder Woman was born as an Amazon and had many powers gifted to her by the mythical gods and goddesses. Her magic lasso was forged from the Magic Girdle of Aphrodite, which had been given to Wonder Woman's mother by the goddess. "It was unbreakable, infinitely stretchable, and could make all who are encircled in it tell the truth."

In the comics, Wonder Woman's lasso inevitably finds its way around the bad guys, imprisoning them and coercing them to tell the truth. But in the real world, it's truth that frees us. One day Jesus was speaking about truth to a crowd that included Pharisees. They were questioning Him, trying to trip Him up.

> To the Jews who had believed him, Jesus said, "If you hold to my teaching, you are really my disciples. Then you will know the truth, and the truth will set you free."
>
> They answered him, "We are Abraham's descendants and have never been slaves of anyone. How can you say that we shall be set free?"
>
> Jesus replied, "Very truly I tell you, everyone who sins is a slave to sin. Now a slave has no permanent

place in the family, but a son belongs to it forever. So if the Son sets you free, you will be free indeed. (John 8:31–36 NIV)

Like Wonder Woman, we can use truth as a powerful weapon. Rather than give in to our natural, sinful selves, we can use truth to bind up the lies in our lives and be set free from them. We do not need to live any longer as slaves to the untruths that may have followed us for years. We have been redeemed, and how precious is that second chance? Accept Jesus' offer: resolve today to allow yourself the gift of freedom from lies.

## A PRAYER

Thank You, Lord God, for the freedom You have given us through the truth of Your Son. Help me remember His supreme sacrifice when I am tempted to sin. Amen.

## TAKE ACTION

- If you have been dishonest with someone, it's time to come clean. Tell that person what you've done and ask for his or her forgiveness.
- Pray for the strength to be honest when it would be so much easier to shade the truth a little bit.

- It's become almost acceptable to cheat on tests these days. Free yourself from the slavery of lies by being honest in all areas of your life.

# 15

# Faith in Others

Morpheus and Trinity, *The Matrix*

> *In You, O LORD, I put my trust;*
> *Let me never be ashamed;*
> *Deliver me in Your righteousness.*

—Psalm 31:1

If you had one person in your life who believed in you when all odds were seemingly against you, count yourself among the fortunate ones. Precious few of us have had the gift of another person who saw something special in us when it seemed the world had turned its back on us. In *The Matrix*, we meet a seemingly average-Joe computer programmer by day, named Thomas Anderson (aka Neo, his hacker name by night), who is about to experience this gift in a powerful way.

Morpheus is the captain of the crew that rescues Neo from the virtual world where everything around him is in reality a computer-generated illusion masking a slavish system in which all humans are used as an electrical energy source and kept imprisoned by an artificial intelligence called "the Matrix." The powerful Morpheus has been on an unrelenting hunt for "the One" who will rescue humanity from the Matrix, and he believes he's found it in Neo. After they pull Neo out of the Matrix's grasp, he turns to his beautiful and strong crew member, Trinity: "We've done it Trinity. We found him."

Trinity replies, "I hope you're right."

"I don't have to hope it. I know it."

Neo, however, is slower to believe in himself than Morpheus is. After all, he has just come from a world where he was simply an anonymous number at a computer programming company. Hardly someone who will save humanity. Morpheus tries to explain it to the bewildered Neo: "I saw you, Neo, and my world changed. You can call it an epiphany, you can call it whatever . . . you want. It doesn't matter. . . . All I can do is believe, Neo, believe that one day you will feel what I felt and know what I know . . . You are the One."

> "You can't be dead, Neo, you can't be, because I love you."
>
> **—TRINITY**

Over time Trinity comes to have faith in the young man, too, but for her own reasons. The Oracle, a wise old lady who speaks prophetically, had told her that she'd fall in love with the One. And since she has fallen in love with Neo . . . well, that confirms for her that he is it.

In a climactic scene that takes place in the virtual

reality world of the Matrix, Neo is shot dead. Back in the real world, Trinity whispers in his ear: "The Oracle, she told me that I'd fall in love and that man, the man I loved, would be the One. You see? You can't be dead, Neo, you can't be, because I love you. You hear me? I love you!"

Because of her faith in him, Neo comes back from death to defeat the Matrix and take his place as "the One."

Our lives are not as dramatic as this movie, of course, but the effect we can have on another person by having faith in that individual can be life-changing in a way a film never could be. You may know someone who desperately needs to have another person express faith in him or her when no one else will. He may not have anyone else in his entire life who has his back.

Maybe it's time to step up and be that person who can make all the difference in someone's life. These are the types of actions that bring joy to God, to see us ministering to each other in His name.

## A PRAYER

Dear Father, thank You for the people You've placed in my life who have had faith in me, even in the darkest hours. Let me be that light for another person. Amen.

# TAKE ACTION

- Identify one person who needs and deserves someone to believe in him or her, and let that individual know that you have faith in him or her, and why.
- If you have young children in your life, write cards letting them know you think they're special—that they matter and that you're proud of them.
- If you've been lucky in life to have someone who pulled for you at a critical juncture— perhaps a teacher, coach, or scout leader—let that special person know today you're thankful for his or her faith in you.

# 16
# Compassion

John Coffey, *The Green Mile*

> *He has made His wonderful works to be remembered;*
> *The LORD is gracious and full of compassion.*
>
> —Psalm 111:4

When we first meet the titanic-sized John Coffey, played by actor Michael Clarke Duncan, he's being led in shackles into the Tennessee State Penitentiary, the latest resident on death row. Convicted of the murders of two girls, the man simply said of the crime, "I couldn't take it back, Boss." *Webster's Dictionary* defines *compassion* as "sympathetic consciousness of others' distress together with a desire to alleviate it." Given what he's done, Coffey certainly doesn't seem to be a likely candidate to be described as "compassionate." What he can fairly be characterized as, though, is a man with a mysterious talent.

We see it when a brutal prison guard, Percy, stomps to death a little mouse, which was a beloved pet to the prisoner Del. Coffey cups the mouse in his huge hands and breathes in deep the air around the mouse—he inhales death. It is not without cost to himself though; Coffey chokes on it, and on hands and knees, with a contorted face, hacks up what he inhaled. Out spews what looks like thousands of tiny flies, which dissipate into the air. To the shock of the other guards, the little rodent's tail begins to twitch, and the creature comes back to life. "I helped Del's mouse . . ." Coffey says softly. "Boss Percy's bad. He mean. He step on Del's mouse. I took it back, though."

> Now they know that Coffey has an unbelievably powerful gift.

Speechless, now they know that Coffey has an unbelievably powerful gift.

It's one thing to save a mouse, but quite another to risk himself for another human. If a mouse's death could cause Coffey to choke so severely, what would saving a person cost him? The answer comes when the warden's wife becomes deathly ill. A brain tumor is killing her, and fast. Will Coffey take the risk for a woman he doesn't even know? We find out when the prison guards do something that could end their careers and send them to prison themselves: they sneak John Coffey out of prison and over to the warden's house to save his wife's life. There Coffey chooses compassion and risks his life to save hers. To top it all off, they discover he hadn't killed the two little girls. He was simply torn up that he couldn't "take back" the murders that someone else had already committed.

The gospel parallels in this story are abundantly clear. We know that when Jesus walked the earth He healed the sick and the lame and raised the dead back to life. John Coffey reminds us in a small way of Jesus when Coffey takes into himself the cancer that is going to kill the warden's wife. He knew when he did it that it would be a serious risk to his own life. How blessed we are that *our* hero is a *real* one who had such compassion for us sinners that He took on our sins and died for us on the cross so that we can experience everlasting life.

Christ knew His whole life that He would pay the ultimate price for His compassion, that it would cost Him great pain, rejection, and a horrific death. But He also knew that He would be obedient to His Father. When you are called to be compassionate, remember the incredible example of our Savior and have a heart that is willing to go where you are needed, to help the person He wants you to help, and to love as He loved.

## A PRAYER

Dear Jesus, thank You for your unending compassion for us. Help me to mirror Your love in my actions. Amen.

# TAKE ACTION

- Consider making a onetime donation to a charitable organization such as Charity: Water (charitywater.org) or Blood:Water Mission (bloodwatermission.com), both of which provide clean water to those who have none.
- Read Psalm 111 to see how God shows His compassion.
- Donate some of your time to a local food bank. The need is always great.
- "Breathe some life" back into a shut-in's world by taking him or her for a wheelchair walk.

# 17

# Independence

Jane Eyre

*Finally, my brethren, be strong in the Lord and in the power of His might. Put on the whole armor of God, that you may be able to stand against the wiles of the devil.*

—Ephesians 6:10–11

Have you ever had a goal and run smack against a brick wall? You're too young to do that, someone told you. Or you're supposedly too old to start something new. Or you've hit a glass ceiling. Or you've been otherwise discriminated against because of your race, gender, or a handicap. Whatever the reason, society can discourage and block you from realizing your dreams.

Charlotte Brontë lived at a time when women were discouraged from having goals outside the home. When she wrote *Jane Eyre* in 1847, it was not exactly prime time for women's independence. In fact, Brontë had to write her novel under a male pseudonym, Currer Bell. Society in nineteenth-century England was completely dominated by men, and it was mostly unheard-of for women to write a book. When Jane Austen published *Sense and Sensibility* in 1811, she was identified as simply "A Lady"; her now-famous name was only attached to her work after her death. And to this day more people recognize Mary Anne Evans by the pseudonym George Eliot than by her given name. Women were expected to tend to home and family, and they were largely considered inferior to men, including their husbands. This was the environment into which Brontë introduced Jane Eyre, a character destined to become one of the most independent women in literature.

We meet Jane as a young orphan forced to live with relatives who despise and mistreat her. Soon she finds herself shipped off to Lowood Institution, a charity school for girls, where she endures hunger and more harsh treatment for six years. Here Jane realizes that she is destined to be impoverished and helpless forever unless she finds a way to become more independent. She advertises her services as a governess and is soon employed at Thornhill, a mansion owned by a Mr. Rochester.

We see signs of Jane's independence even while she is being swept off her feet by Rochester. He tries to shower her with gifts; she refuses to accept them. He can't believe that after she marries him she wants to continue working as governess to his ward, but she insists on retaining the position.

Then the biggest test of her backbone: she discovers that the man she loves is already married, and to a lunatic at that! The woman is being kept in an attic room in the mansion. And the heartsick man adores Jane so much he begs her to stay with him regardless. He pledges his fidelity to her and asks for hers in return.

"Why are you silent, Jane?"

"I was experiencing an ordeal," she answered, "a hand of fiery iron grasped my vitals. Terrible moment: full of struggle, blackness, burning! Not a human being that ever lived could wish to be loved better than I was loved, and him who thus loved me I absolutely worshipped: and I must renounce love and idol. One drear word comprised my intolerable duty—Depart! . . . Mr. Rochester, I will *not* be yours."

Jane is strong and does leave Thornhill, and she makes her way in the world alone and independent once more—until fate brings her back to Rochester a year later. His mad wife has been killed in a fire that destroyed not only Thornhill, but Rochester's sight as well. He and Jane are reunited, and Jane is finally married to her love.

> "Depart! . . . Mr. Rochester, I will *not* be yours."
>
> —JANE EYRE

When life hands you a blow, how do you respond? Do you give up and go with the flow, do you wait for someone to rescue you, or do you pray to God, put on His armor, and move forward? Brontë wrote her novels despite the fact that she was a female in Victorian England. Jane Eyre found the strength to do the right thing and leave Rochester and become independent once more. We, too, can choose to take the braver path and step out in faith.

## A PRAYER

Dear Lord, when I feel stymied by people or events, help me remember that You give me the wisdom to know what to do. Thank You for your armor so that I can be strong in your power. Amen.

## TAKE ACTION

- Is there something you've always wanted to do deep in your heart but felt that you'd be rejected? Identify one thing like that in your life. Pray, and then take a small step toward your goal today.
- If you know someone who is facing a tough decision whether or not to strike out on his or her own, help that person create a balance sheet of pros and cons so he or she can make the best choice.

# 18

# Integrity

Atticus Finch, *To Kill a Mockingbird*

> *The Lord God is a sun and shield;*
> *The Lord will give grace and glory;*
> *No good thing will He withhold*
> *From those who walk uprightly.*
>
> **—Psalm 84:11**

It seems as if the whole town has shown up for the trial. A black man is charged with raping a white woman, and white attorney Atticus Finch is charged with defending the accused, Tom Robinson. The fact that Finch delivers a rousing defense doesn't win him any white favor in that small, Depression-era Alabama town depicted in Harper Lee's classic novel, *To Kill a Mockingbird*.

"Scout," says Atticus to his young daughter after a particularly ugly ribbing she's taken at school,

A scene from the play *To Kill a Mockingbird*, performed in Monroeville, Alabama

It's not fair for you and Jem [Atticus's son], I know that, but sometimes we have to make the best of things, and the way we conduct ourselves when the chips are down—well, all I can say is, when you and Jem are grown, maybe you'll look back on this with some compassion and some feeling that I didn't let you down. This case, Tom Robinson's case, is something that goes to the essence of a man's conscience—Scout, I couldn't go to church and worship God if I didn't try to help that man . . . [B]efore I can live with other folks I've got to live with myself.

Atticus was a man of integrity during a time in the Deep South when it could cost your life to stand for your principles.

Centuries earlier, three men had to stand up for their principles at the risk of their lives. Their names were Shadrach, Meshach, and Abed-Nego. The king who captured them had set up a golden idol and demanded that everyone bow down and worship it. He was infuriated when the three Israelites refused. "Is it true, Shadrach, Meshach, and Abed-Nego, that you do not serve my gods or worship the gold image which I have set up? Now if . . . you fall down and worship the image which I have made, good! But if you do not worship, you shall be cast immediately into the midst of a burning fiery furnace. And who is the god who will deliver you from my hands?" (Dan. 3:14–15).

They answered, "O Nebuchadnezzar, we have no need to answer you in this matter. If that is the case, our God whom we serve is able to deliver us from the burning fiery furnace, and He will deliver us from your hand, O king. But if not, let it be known to you, O king, that we do not serve your gods, nor will we worship the gold image which you have set up" (vv. 16–18). And indeed they were cast into the fire. However, they did not die. Instead they walked about unharmed. The king declared that from then on no one should speak amiss of their God, and he promoted them within his kingdom.

> "The one thing that doesn't abide by majority rule is a person's conscience."
>
> **—ATTICUS FINCH**

It doesn't always work out well when we stand up for what we believe in. Atticus knew that he had to do what was right, even when his children were taunted at school, and he was threatened by the accuser's father. Shadrach and friends certainly didn't know they would be rescued by God, but they were willing to go into the fire anyway. Are you willing to "step into the fire" to defend something you believe in, regardless of the personal cost to you? Large issue or small, remember what Atticus Finch said: "The one thing that doesn't abide by majority rule is a person's conscience."

## A PRAYER

Dear God, sometimes I just go along to get along. It's easier. Please help me to recognize when I'm doing that and to stand up for what's right when it really counts, even in the small things. Amen.

## TAKE ACTION

- How are you with integrity? How strong is your instinct for determining what's right and acting on it? Concentrate on and pray for building up this character strength.
- Become a "people watcher." Choose your friends based on their level of integrity, and encourage greater integrity among those you know.

# 19
# Fearlessness

Indiana Jones, *Raiders of the Lost Ark*

*God is strong, and he wants you strong. So take everything the Master has set out for you, well-made weapons of the best materials. And put them to use so you will be able to stand up to everything the Devil throws your way.*

**—Ephesians 6:10–11** MSG

The natives are hot on the heels of Indiana Jones as he makes a run for the bush plane waiting for him on the river, deep in the Andes rain forest. His pilot, Jacques, revs the plane forward just as Indy scrambles inside and drops into a seat. But his triumph is short-lived when he discovers he shares the space with a huge boa constrictor, Jacques's pet.

"Don't mind him. That's Reggie. Wouldn't hurt a soul."

"I can't stand snakes," replies Indy.

He gets no sympathy from Jacques: "The world's full of them, you know."

"I hate them," reiterates Jones.

Unfortunately for Indy, it won't be the last time he has to face what he fears the most. Later in the movie *Raiders of the Lost Ark*, he will have to deal with them again, in spades.

"Why snakes?" asks Indy. "Why did it have to be snakes? Anything else."

Now, fast-forward a few scenes. He and his friend Sallah have just uncovered the buried chamber called "the Well of Souls," where the long-lost Ark of the Covenant is hidden. Indy drops his torch to the floor thirty feet below, sees a slithering, hissing mass, and turns pale. The floor is covered in undulating knots and whorls of asps, one of the world's deadliest snakes.

"Why snakes?" asks Indy. "Why did it have to be snakes? Anything else."

Have you ever had a "snake moment," like Indy? Everyone has something that causes almost irrational fear. For you it may be spiders, public speaking, making a mistake at work, or getting stuck in an elevator. Perhaps it's something more serious, such as something happening to your kids, a bad fight with your parents, or losing your spouse to death or divorce. You think, *Just don't let it be* that. Anything *else!*

As Christians, we don't have to live like that. For us to live in fear absolutely delights Satan, because it is just the opposite of what our Savior wants for us. In fact, Paul call us to be strong in the Lord and in His mighty power. "Put on the full armor of God, so that you can take your stand against the devil's schemes. For our struggle is not against flesh and blood, but against the rulers, against the authorities, against the powers of this dark world and against the spiritual forces of evil in the heavenly realms" (Eph. 6:11–12 NIV).

Did you notice that? We are fighting against the devil's schemes all the time! He loves to see us afraid, to cause us to give up on our dreams, to thwart us when we do good in the world. He knows that the fully armored Christ follower is a formidable foe. "Therefore put on the full armor of God," Paul continued, "so that when the day of evil comes, you may be able to stand your ground, and after you have done everything, to stand" (v. 13).

Next time that "snake moment" threatens to take away your peace, remember to put on the full armor of God so that you can stand firm.

## A PRAYER

Dear Jesus, I know the forces of evil love it when I let them destroy my peace. Please help me remember to put on Your armor every day so I can stand firm against fear.

## TAKE ACTION

- Read Ephesians 6:10–18 to find out about each piece of your armor.
- Pray for strength to overcome your fears. And pray for people you know who are fighting fears, that they may find peace through faith and the powerful Word of God.
- Stand strong against your fears. For example, if you are asked to make a public presentation because you are the most qualified, don't say no because you fear public speaking. Confront your fears; you'll find you can conquer them.

# 20

# Coolness Under Pressure

James Bond, *Goldfinger*

> *And the peace of God, which transcends*
> *all understanding, will guard your hearts*
> *and your minds in Christ Jesus.*
>
> —Philippians 4:7 NIV

He is strapped to a gold table, and the laser beam slices ever closer, threatening to cut him in two. What is 007 to do? Mr. Goldfinger and his minions have him at their mercy, and there appears to be no escape. "I think you've made your point, Goldfinger. Thank you for the demonstration," Bond quipps.

"Choose your next witticism carefully, Mr. Bond. It may be your last," replies Goldfinger.

Oh, that we could all be so smooth under pressure as James Bond. We know he'll somehow always make it out of impossible situations. This one is no exception.

Sean Connery in *Goldfinger*, directed by Guy Hamilton (Beverly Hills: United Artists, 1964)

"You're forgetting one thing! If I fail to report, 008 replaces me! . . . He knows what I know!"

"You know nothing, Mr. Bond!"

"Operation Grand Slam, for instance!" says Bond, reminding Goldfinger of a top-secret gold-smuggling operation.

"Two words you may have overheard which cannot possibly have any significance to you or anyone in your organization."

As they parry words, the laser beam continues to slice through the table, coming perilously close to Bond's torso. Still he keeps his cool.

"Can you afford to take that chance?" he asks Goldfinger.

Wouldn't it be great if we had James Bond's smoothness, his unflappability, in all circumstances?

Exasperated, Goldfinger snaps his fingers, and the man running the laser beam cuts it off at the last possible millisecond. "You are quite right, Mr. Bond. You are worth more to me alive."

Once again James Bond, the consummate cool guy, escapes certain death. Wouldn't it be great if we had his smoothness, his unflappability, in all circumstances? Well, as Christians, we actually are directed not to be anxious in anything. So when you are worried all the time and fretting rather than being calm and proactive, you are not in the will of God. In Philippians, Paul tells us to rejoice in the Lord always and to let our gentleness be evident to all. "Do not be anxious about anything, but in every situation, by prayer and petition, with thanksgiving, present your requests to God. And the peace of God, which transcends all understanding, will guard your hearts and your minds in Christ Jesus" (4:6–7 NIV).

What an amazing promise. Lay claim to it today and discover the peace that can be yours.

## A PRAYER

Dear Jesus, most of the time the last thing I feel is peaceful. Forgive me for forgetting to come to You in prayer and claim the peace that You promised me. Thank You for this gift that comes only from You. Amen.

## TAKE ACTION

- Today, try claiming the promises of Philippians 4. Take everything to God in prayer, and discover what peace that can bring you.
- Consciously model your thoughts on Philippians 4:8–9.
- Take a few minutes every day this week to incorporate some peaceful time into your life, whether it be a walk through the neighborhood, talking over coffee with a friend, or losing yourself in a novel or book of poetry.

# 21
# Protecting Others

Jake Sully, *Avatar*

> *But let all those rejoice who put their trust in You;*
> *Let them ever shout for joy, because You defend them;*
> *Let those also who love Your name*
> *Be joyful in You.*
> *For You, O LORD, will bless the righteous;*
> *With favor You will surround him as with a shield.*

—Psalm 5:11–12

The Avatar Program looks, on the surface, to be a benign scientific foray into another planet's culture. But the real power behind the throne, Colonel Quaritch, has other ideas. The local Na'vi inhabitants, the Omaticaya tribe, are living on top of a deposit of priceless unobtanium, and he is determined to mine it, no matter the cost to the natives.

That's where Jake Sully comes in. When he is linked into his avatar, the wheelchair-bound marine can appear as a native and speak to them, and that is just what Quaritch needs. Through Sully, he can get intel on how to defeat them. "I need you to learn about these savages, gain their trust. Find out how I can force their cooperation, or hit 'em hard if they don't. Maybe you can keep some of my boys from going home [handicapped] like you. Or bagged-and-tagged."

Sully nods. "That sounds real good, Colonel."

As Sully spends time with the Omaticaya—and the beautiful Neytiri in particular—he begins to appreciate their gentle culture, and eventually he comes to love them and feels he's become one of them. Before he realizes his loyalty has changed, though, Jake reluctantly gives Quaritch the intel he needs to threaten their most holy place, the Tree of Souls. Things get uncomfortable with the colonel, who is itching to get the locals off their land. It soon becomes obvious they will not leave of their own will: "They're not going to give up their home—they're not gonna make a deal. For what? Lite beer and shopping channel? There's nothing we have that they want. We're a horror to them. We're the monsters from space," Jake says.

> "They're not going to give up their home—they're not gonna make a deal. For what? Lite beer and shopping channel?"
>
> —JAKE SULLY

Jake's protective instinct comes out finally, and he decides to do whatever it takes to prevent Quaritch and his troops from driving out the natives. Jake gathers all the tribes of the Na'vi to fight against the modern warfare capabilities of Quaritch's forces. "Ride out, as fast as the wind can carry you; tell the other clans to come. Tell them *Toruk Makto* calls to them. Fly now with me, brothers and sisters! Fly! And we will show the Sky People that this is our land!" Against all odds, the Na'vi win the victory and save their planet.

If you were a fortunate child, you had parents who were protective of you, as Jake Sully was of the Na'vi. Perhaps now you have children of your own, with whom you feel that same strong bond. It's only natural you desire to keep your loved ones from danger. And it's frustrating, and terrifying at times, when you realize that no matter what you do, you can never keep them 100 percent safe from what's out there. But no matter how much you love your family, God loves them more, and they're in His hands. Remember the words of the psalmist when he wrote in Psalm 61,

> *Hear my cry, O God;*
> *Attend to my prayer.*
> *From the end of the earth I will cry to You,*
> *When my heart is overwhelmed;*
> *Lead me to the rock that is higher than I.*
> *For You have been a shelter for me,*
> *A strong tower from the enemy.*
> *I will abide in Your tabernacle forever;*
> *I will trust in the shelter of Your wings. Selah (vv. 1–4)*

For those days when you just want to wrap your arms around and protect your loved ones, allow God to be your family's rock, your shelter, your strong tower, and trust in Him.

## A PRAYER

Lord God, thank You for loving my family more than even I can. Help me trust that You'll take care of them. Amen.

## TAKE ACTION

- Memorize Psalm 61 for times when you need to remember God is your strength.
- When you catch yourself being overprotective as a parent, try to remind yourself that God loves your children more than you can imagine.

# 22
# Wisdom

Yoda, *Star Wars Episode V: The Empire Strikes Back*

*The wise mind will know the time and the way.*

—**Ecclesiastes 8:5** NRSV

He is a tiny and wrinkled hero, but the little creature is a Jedi Master. Yoda's appearance reminds us that heroes can come in unexpected packages. Despite his stature, he possesses the wisdom of the ages, yet when Luke Skywalker first sees him, he dismisses him. This diminutive fellow could not be the great Jedi he was looking for, could he? When Luke is finally convinced of Yoda's identity, though, he has to convince him that he is ready for training. He needs Jedi training from Yoda, and he needs it now!

"Ready, are you?" Yoda observes. "What know you of ready? For eight hundred years have I trained Jedi. My own counsel will I keep on who is to be trained! A Jedi must have the deepest commitment, the most serious mind. . . . Hmph. Adventure. Heh! Excitement. Heh! A Jedi craves

Yoda in *Star Wars Episode V: The Empire Strikes Back*, directed by Irvin Kershner (LucasFilms Ltd., 1980)

not these things. You are reckless!" Luke looks down. He knows it is true.

Later Yoda explains, "A Jedi's strength flows from the Force. But beware of the dark side. Anger . . . fear . . . aggression. The dark side of the Force are they. Easily they flow, quick to join you in a fight. If once you start down the dark path, forever will it dominate your destiny, consume you it will, as it did Obi-Wan's apprentice."

"Vader. Is the dark side stronger?" asks Luke.

"No . . . no . . . no," the wise trainer replies. "Quicker, easier, more seductive."

"But how am I to know the good side from the bad?"

"You will know. When you are calm, at peace. Passive. A Jedi uses the Force for knowledge and defense, never for attack."

King Solomon, whose wisdom is found in Proverbs, knew we would have a hard time discerning good from evil, which can appear "quicker, easier, more seductive." Like Luke, we doubt our ability to tell them apart sometimes. How do we know the difference?

> *Trust in the LORD with all your heart,*
> *And lean not on your own understanding;*
> *In all your ways acknowledge Him,*
> *And He shall direct your paths.*
> *Do not be wise in your own eyes;*

*Fear the L*ORD *and depart from evil.*
*It will be health to your flesh,*
*And strength to your bones. (Prov. 3:5–8)*

In this scripture we are essentially being told not to trust ourselves without the backing of the Holy Spirit. We are to trust in Him for discernment in all things, not try a solo act. Do you long for a wise heart? Begin at the basics, in the Word, and you'll have a good start:

*The fear of the L*ORD *is the beginning of wisdom,*
*And the knowledge of the Holy One is understand-*
*ing. (Prov. 9:10)*

The less you depend on your own knowledge and the more you depend on the Word of God, the more you'll find a heart bent toward wisdom.

## A PRAYER

Dear Lord, help me to know Your Word and Your heart so much that I can be wise. Guide me to a confident heart that can discern good from evil. Amen.

## TAKE ACTION

- Dedicate this month to reading and meditating on Proverbs.

- One of the most dangerous things a Christian can do is try to rely solely on his own wisdom—to go it alone—when dealing with sin. Pray this week to allow the Holy Spirit to work within you to help you discern what may be unhealthy in your life. Reach out for help if necessary.

# 23

# Intrepidness

## Huckleberry Finn

> *"'You will not need to fight in this battle. Position yourselves, stand still and see the salvation of the LORD, who is with you, O Judah and Jerusalem!' Do not fear or be dismayed; tomorrow go out against them, for the LORD is with you."*
>
> **—2 Chronicles 20:17**

"It felt good gettin' back on the river. Other places feel so cramped and smothered, but the river don't. I always feel warm and safe and free on the river," said Huck Finn. He and his escaped slave friend, Jim, were having more adventure than they'd signed on for as they journeyed down the muddy Mississippi on their raft, but the river still represented freedom to both of the intrepid travelers.

In Disney's *The Adventures of Huck Finn*, we first see Huck choose the path of fearless adventure when he fakes his own death to escape his murderous father. "Now that

HUCKLEBERRY FINN.

Frontispiece in *Adventures of Huckleberry Finn* (Tom Sawyer's Comrade), by Mark Twain (New York: Charles L. Webster and Co., 1885, c1884)

I was dead," he explains, "I could do what I wanted and go where I wanted, and neither Pap nor Miss Watson [the widow who had taken him in] would ever try to follow me." He continues his dauntless ways when he chooses to pair up with Jim, who has the law after him for escaping slavery and for supposedly killing Huck.

After their raft is crushed by an oncoming steamboat, Huck swims to shore and is taken in by a wealthy family. The family also claims ownership of Jim, who has washed up on shore, too, but his lot is not as lucky as Huck's: he is destined for the cotton fields and an overseer who whips him.

Huck is momentarily taken in by how well he himself is being treated and turns his back on Jim. But when he sees the red stripes on Jim's back from a whipping, he repents and apologizes to his friend. When the family is wiped out by another family with whom they were feuding, Huck and Jim take off on the river again.

In their last, and most fateful, adventure, the duo is forced to fall in with a couple of tricksters named the King and the Duke, who are trying to fool a family into believing they are the long-lost brothers of Peter Wilks, a wealthy man who has just died. But when they are found out as frauds, Jim is imprisoned as an escaped slave and is to be sent north for hanging.

Desperate, Huck has to figure out how to spring his friend. The answer comes when the sheriff is distracted by the noisy shouts of the townspeople as they find out they've all been duped by the brothers. Huck is able to steal the keys to the prison from the sheriff's belt and free Jim. It's off to the river again.

At the end of the movie, Huck and Jim don't make it to freedom. Instead Jim is captured and almost hanged, until one of the young Wilks ladies rescues him from the noose. Huck's intrepid ways seem to be nearing an end when the widow Douglas decides to take him in and "civilize" him. That just doesn't appeal to the young whippersnapper, and he runs off again, no doubt heading for the great Mississippi, where he feels warm and safe and free.

*Merriam-Webster's Dictionary* defines *intrepid* as "characterized by resolute fearlessness, fortitude, and endurance." Do you have something in your heart, like Huck's, that helps you feel fearless? Even if you don't, you, too, can be intrepid. With crime, war, and terrorism rampant, it seems the world is a place worthy of being feared. But the Lord tells us not to be dismayed when we're against great odds, because He is with us. The psalmist wrote many songs about being afraid, and in perhaps his most famous psalm, the twenty-third, he muses:

> *Yea, though I walk through the valley of the shadow of death,*
> *I will fear no evil;*
> *For You are with me;*
> *Your rod and Your staff, they comfort me. (v. 4)*

God does not want His children to live with a spirit of fear. He wants us to step boldly out in faith, strong in His Word. Remembering this in times of trial will keep us strong in the face of whatever evil comes our way.

## A PRAYER

Dear Lord, sometimes I don't feel very intrepid. Please help me recognize those moments when it's wise to stand up and move out with courage and confidence, and remind me that when You are with me, no one can prevail against me. Amen.

## TAKE ACTION

- If you are being called to fearlessness, first determine through prayer if it is a call from God. And if it is, take a step forward.
- Missionaries are God's forward line, and it requires a special kind of bravery. Call a church today, and ask if you can send something to help someone on a mission by providing a donation or a letter of encouragement.
- Recognize that our young people, like Huck, are sometimes the ones answering the call of God in the most intrepid ways. Pray

for one of them today, that she or he would be encouraged and remain fearless, bold, and undaunted. And if you are one of these young and intrepid people, know that you are appreciated and blessed.

# 24

# Honor

General Maximus Decimus Meridius, *Gladiator*

> *"If anyone serves Me, let him follow Me; and where I am, there My servant will be also. If anyone serves Me, him My Father will honor."*
>
> —John 12:26

"Brothers, what we do in life echoes in eternity," General Maximus Decimus Meridius, played by Russell Crowe, reminds his army before they set out to fight the Germans. They follow him into yet another victory that day. And as he walks through the debris of the battlefield afterward with Caesar Marcus Aurelius, the soldiers cheer the two as they pass.

"It is you, Maximus. They honor you," Marcus Aurelius tells him.

Maximus has spent more than two years fighting with these men, and he's earned their love and respect—the honor they show him. After the battles, instead of secluding himself in the luxury of his tent, he has the habit of walking among the men in their camp, greeting and congratulating them as they rest, eat, and sharpen their swords. This has only made them more loyal.

> "It is you, Maximus. They honor you," Marcus Aurelius tells the general.

He is also honored by Marcus Aurelius, who tells him, "I want you to become the protector of Rome after I die. I will empower you, to one end alone, to give power back to the people of Rome and end the corruption that has crippled it. Will you accept this great honor that I have offered?"

Maximus replies, "With all my heart, no."

"Maximus," Marcus Aurelius says, "that is why it must be you."

When the treacherous Commodus, Marcus Aurelius's son, finds out that the power of Rome has been bequeathed to Maximus instead of to him, he murders his father, has Maximus's family killed, and tries to have Maximus himself slain. Maximus survives and escapes Commodus's men, however, only to be captured and sold into slavery to a man named Proximo, who owns gladiators. Maximus lives only for revenge against Commodus.

As a gladiator, Maximus's natural leadership abilities begin to rise again, and some of the other fighters who had served under him are still loyal to him. On the arena floor his group is supposed to lose against the other gladiators, who ride in chariots. He asks the men with him, "Anyone here been in the army?"

"Yes," says one.

"I served with you in Vindobona," says another. The honor Maximus has earned as a general will serve him well here.

"You can help me," Maximus tells all the men. "Whatever comes out of these gates, we have a better chance of survival if we work together. Do you understand? We stay together, we survive . . . Come together . . . lock your shields, stay as one . . . hold as one." Against all odds his ragtag team of gladiators comes together to win the arena battle.

Finally Maximus gets the chance to fight Commodus, who cheats by stabbing him before the match. But as he dies, Maximus, fighting with honor, kills Commodus.

*Honor* is a good name for public esteem. Are you held in honor? In 2 Timothy, Paul explained to a young man that "in a great house there are not only vessels of gold and silver, but also of wood and clay, some for honor and some for dishonor. Therefore if anyone cleanses himself from the latter, he will be a vessel for honor, sanctified and useful for the Master, prepared for every good work" (2:20–21). We are not only to flee youthful lusts, but also to pursue righteousness, faith, love, and peace (v. 22). By doing these things, we become the "vessels of gold and silver"

Paul spoke of. It's a different path to honor than that of Maximus, to be sure, but the end result is the same: what we do in life will echo in eternity.

## A PRAYER

Dear God, I want to be a person of honor. Please guide my steps so that I am useful to You, a vessel of gold or silver, and not of wood or clay. Amen.

## TAKE ACTION

- Consider honoring the POWs/MIAs from our wars with your own moment of silence this morning.
- Write down ways you can pursue righteousness, faith, love, and peace this week.

# 25
# Determination

Ellen Ripley, *Aliens*

> "Ask, and it will be given to you; seek, and you
> will find; knock, and it will be opened to you."
>
> —Matthew 7:7

Accompanied by a team of Colonial Marines, Ellen Ripley has landed on the Acheron colony on a faraway planetoid where all the people have mysteriously disappeared. Early in the movie they discover the lone survivor, a traumatized little girl named Newt, who quickly becomes beloved by the tough-shelled Ripley. Newt doesn't speak much at first, other than to tell Ripley about her family, "They're dead."

What follows, a series of horrific attacks by aliens, takes out almost all the soldiers. Ripley, determined to save little Newt, protects her in attack after attack. As she and Corporal Hicks, the lone surviving marine, flee through the air ducts, Newt falls and disappears down into the depths of the station, crying for Ripley the whole way.

"Stay where you are, Newt!" Ripley yells down. "We're coming!"

Unfortunately, by the time she gets to where Newt has fallen, the little girl has been taken by an alien, destined for the fate of the rest of the colonists. Most people would give up at that point, but not Ripley.

"No, no!" she cries to Hicks. "She's alive, she's alive!"

"All right! I believe you! She's alive!" the injured Hicks yells as he pulls her away from the water where Newt was just moments before.

But Hicks is too wounded to help Ripley. So she ventures alone into the heart of the aliens' territory, where, against all odds, she locates and rescues Newt by taking on the queen of the aliens right in her lair.

Anyone who sees Ellen Ripley in action admires her determination to save the precious little girl who comes under her care. While we won't be called to fight space aliens, chances are that sometime in life we will be called to be equally as determined as Ripley to do something important. Will we persevere or fall short? God tells us that in every such situation we are to ask, seek, and knock, and good things will be given to us (Matt. 7:7). When you find yourself in a precarious situation that calls for your unwavering determination, remember you—unlike Ripley—are not alone in the fight. You have a Father who loves you and will not fail—all you have to do is ask.

# A PRAYER

Dear Lord, please help me remember that when I must find it within myself to be determined, I can call on You for help. I give thanks that I never have to go it alone. Amen.

# TAKE ACTION

- Are you being called to have determination to accomplish something? Write down your goal. You are statistically much more likely to be successful if you put it on paper.
- Pray daily, asking, seeking, and calling on God to help you maintain your sense of determination to reach your goal.
- There is someone in your life who has a difficult goal to reach. Encourage that person with a Facebook comment, a note, or a compliment about how proud you are that he or she has not given up.

# 26
# Encouragement

Woody, *Toy Story*

*In your relationships with one another,*
*have the same mindset as Christ Jesus.*

—Philippians 2:5 NIV

"Hey, Etch! Draw!" calls out Woody. They each whip around like a Wild West gunfighter. The Etch-a-Sketch gets the drop on Woody, however, by quickly drawing a gun on its screen. Woody pretends to be shot.

"Oh! You got me again, Etch! You've been working on that draw. Fastest knobs in the West," Woody tells him.

Woody may only be a toy cowboy, but he's also a natural leader, and he exudes encouragement for those who follow him.

A little bit later in the movie *Toy Story*, the toys are upset because their owner, little Andy, is having a birthday party. Will they be replaced by something newer and "cooler"?

"I'm not worried. You shouldn't be worried," Woody assures them.

Slinky Dog replies, "If Woody says it's all right, then, well, darn it, it's good enough for me. Woody has never steered us wrong before."

"Hey, listen, no one's getting replaced. This is Andy we're talking about. It doesn't matter how much we're played with. What matters is that we're here for Andy when he needs us. That's what we're made for. Right?" Woody's words set them all at ease.

But Woody's bright outlook is later put to the test, when he and fellow toy Buzz Lightyear end up in the neighbor's house, captured by Sid, a boy who tortures his toys for fun. While they plot their escape, Buzz sees a commercial of himself on Sid's TV and realizes, to his shock, that he is *not* an intergalactic warrior, but instead just a toy. The despair of it renders Buzz numb and depressed. He doesn't even care anymore that he and Woody are in the hands of an evil little kid. Woody tries to talk him around to helping with the escape plans.

"Oh, come on, Buzz. I . . . Buzz, I can't do this without you. I need your help."

"I can't help. I can't help anyone."

"Why, sure you can, Buzz. You can get me out of here, and then I'll get that rocket off you, and we'll make a break for Andy's house."

"Andy's house. Sid's house. What's the difference?" the despondent Buzz responds.

"Oh, Buzz, you've had a big fall. You must not be thinking clearly."

"No, Woody, for the first time I *am* thinking clearly. You were right all along. I'm not a Space Ranger. I'm just a toy. A stupid little insignificant toy."

"Whoa, hey—wait a minute," encourages Woody. "Being a toy is a lot better than being a Space Ranger."

"Yeah, right."

"No, it is," continues Woody. "Look, over in that house is a kid who thinks you are the greatest, and it's not because you're a Space Ranger, pal; it's because you're a *toy*! You are *his* toy."

"But why would Andy want me?"

"Why would Andy want you?! Look at you! You're a Buzz Lightyear. Any other toy would give up his moving parts just to be you.

> "Look at you! You're a Buzz Lightyear. Any other toy would give up his moving parts just to be you."
>
> **—SHERIFF WOODY PRIDE**

You've got wings, you glow in the dark, you talk, your helmet does that—that *whoosh* thing—you are a *cool* toy."

At the same time Woody is encouraging him, Buzz sees Andy's name written on the sole of his foot and realizes just how important he is to the boy. The escape is on!

It's amazing what power a few words of encouragement can have. You've felt it in your own life, and you've probably gifted someone else with it as well. Scripture tells us just how important it is: "Therefore if you have any encouragement from being united with Christ, if any comfort from his love, if any common sharing in the Spirit, if any tenderness and compassion, then make my joy complete by being like-minded, having the same love, being one in spirit and of one mind" (Phil. 2:1–2 NIV). Encouraging one another is to be one of our purposes when we are in communion. We are to value others above ourselves and look to the interests of others (Phil. 2:3).

Look for ways in your life to encourage others and show them their value to you and to the people around them. Even in difficult times, you can determine not to let yourself get dragged down. Instead be a hero and show Christ's love by shining the light on the value of others. Remind them that—like Andy's name on Buzz's foot—they have Christ's name written on their hearts. He claims them for His own and adores them.

## A PRAYER

Dear God, when things are rough, I often forget to be an encourager to others. Please help me remember Your name is on the heart of each and every person. Allow me to shine a light on those hearts. Amen.

## TAKE ACTION

- List three to five people in your life who need encouragement and act on that list this week, whether it's writing a note, making a phone call, or delivering a meal.
- On a scale of 1 to 10, rate yourself on how well you encourage people. Determine how you can better look to the interests of others.
- Memorize Philippians 2:3–4: "Do nothing out of selfish ambition or vain conceit. Rather, in humility value others above yourselves, not looking to your own interests but each of you to the interests of the others" (NIV).

# 27

# Courage

> *"Be strong and of good courage, do not fear*
> *nor be afraid . . . for the LORD your God,*
> *He is the One who goes with you. He will*
> *never leave you nor forsake you."*
>
> **—Deuteronomy 31:6**

Of all the four sisters in Louisa May Alcott's novel *Little Women*, Josephine (Jo for short) is the adventurous one. She is the tomboy who writes marvelous plays full of action and villains and derring-do that she and her sisters perform in the attic. Jo devours novels and dreams of becoming a writer someday, but she chafes under the restrictions of women in her 1860s culture. One day she and her mother, whom they all call Marmee, have a heart-to-heart:

"You asked me the other day what my wishes were. I'll tell you one of them, Marmee," she begins, as they sit together, alone. "I want to go away somewhere this winter for a change."

Her mother looks up quickly, as if the words suggest a double meaning. "Why, Jo?"

With her eyes on her work, Jo answers soberly, "I want something new. I feel restless and anxious to be seeing, doing, and learning more than I am. I brood too much over my own small affairs, need stirring up, so as I can be spared this winter, I'd like to hop a little way and try my wings."

"Where will you hop?"

"To New York. I had a bright idea yesterday, and this is it. You know Mrs. Kirke wrote to you for some respectable young person to teach her children and sew. It's rather hard to find just the thing, but I think I should suit if I tried."

> The path to a dream is fraught with uncertainties and potential failure. It requires a strong determination to finish well. And it requires something else: courage.

Marmee is gracious and knows her little bird needs to venture out of the nest, and so she consents to this grand adventure, and off Jo goes.

In New York, Jo finds her first success as a writer of stories for the newspaper, and there she meets the man who will one day become her husband, Friederich Bhaer. It is a glorious time in her life. And finally, when she goes back home, she has the courage to write something unlike anything she's written before: her first novel, *Little Women*.

Are you like Jo? Is there an adventure you've been thinking of diving into? Perhaps you want to step out of your comfort zone and try something new. The path to a dream is fraught with uncertainties and potential failure. It requires a strong determination to finish well. And it requires something else: courage.

Do you stand on Deuteronomy 31:6? "Be strong and of good courage, do not fear nor be afraid . . . for the LORD your God, He is the One who goes with you. He will never leave you nor forsake you." Along your path you will run into roadblocks, but with courage you can overcome them, and the final goal is so worth it!

## A PRAYER

Dear Jesus, today I'm thinking about trying something new, but I'm afraid. Please help me to have faith that You go with me and will not forsake me. Amen.

## TAKE ACTION

- What new venture have you been thinking about? Write it down and pray about it this week—let this be a nudge to take the first big step toward something new and exciting.

- Check out OperationShoeBox.com for great ways to support our courageous troops, such as sending personal hygiene items and sports equipment. And Treat The Troops (www .treatthetroops.org) can help you get cookies to our troops overseas.
- Read 1 Samuel 17, especially verses 34 through 37, to learn the details of David's courageous stand against Goliath.

# 28
# Bearing Burdens

Samwise Gamgee, *The Lord of the Rings*

*"If you love Me, keep My commandments. And I will*
*pray the Father, and He will give you another Helper,*
*that He may abide with you forever—the Spirit*
*of truth, whom the world cannot receive, because*
*it neither sees Him nor knows Him; but you know*
*Him, for He dwells with you and will be in you. I*
*will not leave you orphans; I will come to you."*

—John 14:15–18

"It's just something Gandalf said . . . 'Don't you lose him, Samwise Gamgee.' And I don't mean to." With these words Samwise, also called Sam, declares his devotion to his friend, Frodo, at the beginning of *Lord of the Rings: The Fellowship of the Ring*. And of all the Fellowship, Sam proves himself the most loyal in their epic journey to the dark and dangerous land of Mordor, where they plan to destroy the ring that could give ultimate power to the evil Sauron.

When Frodo is stabbed by a Ringwraith, it is Sam who never leaves his side as he recovers from the almost-fatal injury. At the time the Fellowship of the Ring is first formed at the Council of Elrond, Sam says, "Mr. Frodo's not going anywhere without me," and consequently becomes one of the nine valiant fighters. At the Falls of Rauros, the members of the Fellowship are separated in battle, but Sam stays with Frodo. He is Frodo's defender who keeps watch as they travel.

Sam not only physically protects Frodo during their trip through the gloomy, barren wasteland; he also is supportive when Frodo is particularly discouraged and ready to give in. "Come, Mr. Frodo!" Samwise cries. "I can't carry it [the ring] for you, but I can carry you and it as well. So up you get! Come on, Mr. Frodo dear! Sam will give you a ride. Just tell him where to go, and he'll go." Another time he lifts Frodo's spirits by reminding him, "There's some good in this world, Mr. Frodo . . . and it's worth fighting for."

> "There's some good in this world, Mr. Frodo . . . and it's worth fighting for."
>
> **—SAMWISE GAMGEE**

More than once on the quest, Sam saves Frodo's very life. When the evil spider, Shelob, tries to kill Frodo, it is Sam who drives her away. And when the orcs capture his friend, it is again Sam who is there to rescue Frodo. It is the two of them who finally see the ring destroyed when the tortured villain Gollum and the ring fall into the lava of Mount Doom.

We're more like Frodo than you may think. In this epic quest that is life, we, too, have Sams, people we stick with through the best of times and the very worst. Instead of being a burden, this is a blessing. Paul instructed the Galatians about this very subject: "Brethren, if a man is overtaken in any trespass, you who are spiritual restore such a one in a spirit of gentleness, considering yourself lest you also be tempted. Bear one another's burdens, and so fulfill the law of Christ" (Gal. 6:1–2).

> We're more like Frodo than you may think. In this epic quest that is life, we, too, have Sams.

Do you have a friend whose burdens you are bearing? Or perhaps you are the person blessed with a friend who is supporting you through a tough time. Either way, you're not alone. First Corinthians reminds us, "Do you not know that you are the temple of God and that the Spirit of God dwells in you?" (3:16). Armed with this knowledge, take comfort in the fact that God loves us so much He never leaves us abandoned to our own devices.

## A PRAYER

Dear God, thank You for the Sams in my life. And when I'm feeling heavy from carrying the burden of a friend, help me remember I am not alone— Your Spirit dwells in me and will give me strength. Amen.

## **TAKE ACTION**

- Read John 14, and tuck it away in your heart for a time when you feel alone.
- Touch base with an old friend who demonstrated devotion to you during a particularly tough and stressful time. Or perhaps it's a new friend doing that right now!

# 29

# Rising to the Occasion

Captain John H. Miller, *Saving Private Ryan*

*He also brought me up out of a horrible pit,*
*Out of the miry clay,*
*And set my feet upon a rock,*
*And established my steps.*

—Psalm 40:2

Have you ever been put into a situation that intimidated you beyond all measure, and you weren't sure you were up to the pressure? Captain John H. Miller, played by Tom Hanks, faced such a challenge in *Saving Private Ryan*. His mission: lead a small group of eight soldiers through enemy lines during World War II, find downed paratrooper Private James Ryan, and bring him safely out of danger. The young soldier's three brothers had fallen, and in what some would say was an army PR move, others an act of mercy, the military desired that the mother should have at least one of her sons saved from death.

During the movie, Captain Miller and his men reach a crisis point. The men are demoralized and angry, threatening to abandon the mission and give up the search for Private Ryan. "I'm going back to fight the . . . war," one says. "I'll spend my life in Leavenworth, if I have to, but I'm not going with you." Another soldier agrees: "I can't say as I understand the logic of it myself, sir." And one argues: "We don't even have a way back, sir, once we do find him. Maybe if we had a tank . . ."

How to turn this around? Captain Miller rises to the occasion. He faces the men and begins to talk calmly and quietly:

I teach high school in Addley, Pennsylvania . . . Back home, I tell someone what I do, they'd say it figures. But here . . . it's a big surprise. I guess I've changed. . . .

I have students. And I think if you were to ask them to describe me, most of them would probably use words like "good" or "kind" or "decent." Words that have no meaning here. Words that I've had to forget in order to survive, and to lead.

Or at least I thought I'd forgotten until this mission came along. And as much as I'd like to turn around and go back . . . those words won't let me.

So now I can't help thinking: what if this is what the whole war's been about for us? What if we look back on this as old men, assuming we live, and figure that saving Private Ryan was the one decent thing we were able to pull out of this whole . . . mess?

Maybe then, we'll have earned the right to go back home and carry on with our lives.

At this, he recaptures his leadership, and the men follow him once again into the search through hell for Private Ryan.

In Psalm 40, King David faced an impossible situation in his life as well, a "horrible pit." He must have felt terrified and despairing while he was going through his time of trial. But he was not alone. God enabled him to rise to the circumstances by setting his feet upon a rock and establishing his steps. The Lord heard David's cry, and He will hear yours. He has promised to listen to our prayers and to lift us out of the mire, as long as we trust Him. Remember when you are struggling, no matter the situation, you are not alone. Trying to rise to the occasion on your own is exhausting. Thank goodness we don't have to do it in our own strength!

> "What if we look back on this as old men, assuming we live, and figure that saving Private Ryan was the one decent thing we were able to pull out of this whole . . . mess?"
> —CAPTAIN JOHN H. MILLER

## A PRAYER

Lord, please be with me when I have to rise to the occasion. Remind me that You will set my feet upon the rock. Amen.

## TAKE ACTION

- Read Psalm 40 to learn about perseverance.
- Rising to the occasion may be something huge or small. If you're up for a big challenge, consider signing up for the Big Brother/Big Sister program. Stepping up to the plate for someone younger than you can change a life.
- If you're in school, ask your guidance counselor if there's anyone who needs a mentor; chances are good that you have exactly what someone else needs.

# 30

# Mastery

Zorro, *The Mask of Zorro*

*Having then gifts differing according to the*
*grace that is given to us, let us use them.*

—Romans 12:6

"When the pupil is ready, the master will appear," explains Don Diego de la Vega to the prostrate Alejandro Murrieta. The drunken Alejandro has just been bested in a sword fight by the older man, and he has no idea what de la Vega is talking about. Alejandro is bent on killing a soldier for the murder of his brother, and this old man stopped him with his sword. It was merciful, really, because Alejandro would have been quickly dispatched by the soldier. "Now, if you want to kill this man," de la Vega continues, "I can help you. And I can teach you how: how to move, how to think, how to take your revenge with honor and live to celebrate it. It will take dedication. It will take time."

Alejandro doesn't know yet that his chance meeting with the older man will change his life. De la Vega is an aged Zorro. He is out for some revenge of his own for the death of his wife twenty years earlier and his own wrongful imprisonment. A younger man to take up the mask of Zorro is just the thing. They have a common enemy.

But they have a long way to go to refine Alejandro's sword-fighting skills. At the beginning of training, in Zorro's cave, "the Fox's Lair," Alejandro takes up his sword.

"Do you know how to use that thing?" de la Vega asks him.

"Yes, the pointy end goes into the other man," replies Alejandro.

"This is going to take some work," says de la Vega.

The two train, train, and train some more. Slowly at first, then up to full speed. Alejandro's skills improve. One day de la Vega says, "Perfect. Do it again." More training, until the student has mastered his craft and is ready to step out and begin their plot of revenge. When the time comes, the young Zorro's gift proves well honed, and he is the victor in every fight. In the end, in true hero fashion, he wins both the day and the girl.

While it may not be sword fighting, each of us has been given gifts, and we, too, are responsible to use them well. Are you honing your gifts until you've mastered them? Some gifts require training, training, and more training—to the point we want to give up. And even when we think they're perfect, we must train some more.

Or perhaps you have a gift that you're not using at all. Scripture tells us we're responsible to put it into practice: "Having then gifts differing according to the grace that is given to us, let us use them: if prophecy, let us prophesy in proportion to our faith; or ministry, let us use it in our ministering; he who teaches, in teaching; he who exhorts, in exhortation; he who gives, with liberality; he who leads, with diligence; he who shows mercy, with cheerfulness" (Rom. 12:6–8).

What gifts do you have? Are you using them in a way that glories our Father?

## A PRAYER

Lord, thank You for the gifts You have given me. Father, I know I am responsible to use them. Please give me the wisdom to know how You would have me share them and how I can best develop them. Amen.

## TAKE ACTION

- Make a list of three to five gifts you have or you believe you have. Then ask a friend or family member to confirm or add to your list. Determine how you intend to master those gifts, and then use them productively.

- Give encouragement and provide your expertise, if any, to someone you know who is working hard to hone a gift.

# 31

# Patience

Mr. Darcy, *Pride and Prejudice*

*I waited patiently for the LORD;*
*And He inclined to me,*
*And heard my cry.*

**—Psalm 40:1**

To Elizabeth Bennett, Mr. Wickham seems twice the man Mr. Darcy is. Darcy has been taciturn and rather rude since she met him at a dance—Elizabeth assumes this is his usual demeanor—while Wickham is always the gentleman, handsome and smooth talking. In fact, poor Wickham has been cheated out of his inheritance by Darcy, at least according to Wickham. In actuality Wickham had gambled away his inheritance and is lying to Elizabeth about it. But instead of defending himself, Darcy patiently holds his tongue.

Again Mr. Darcy's character comes under attack when Elizabeth finds out Darcy has talked his best friend, Mr. Bingley, out of marrying Elizabeth's beloved sister Jane.

Darcy is convinced that Jane hasn't returned Bingley's affections, and he's only been trying to spare the feelings of Bingley. But that doesn't matter to Elizabeth, who is livid with him to the point she refuses to accept his hand in marriage.

> Are you more like Elizabeth, quick to judge and easy to anger, or more like Mr. Darcy, patiently holding your tongue, even when things seem unfair?

In fact, for most of Jane Austen's *Pride and Prejudice*, Mr. Darcy patiently puts up with Elizabeth being angry with him despite the fact that none of her bad temper is deserved. In his own time, he corrects her misimpressions of him, restoring Jane and Bingley's relationship and saving Elizabeth's family from shame when the youngest sister runs off with wastrel Mr. Wickham. Mr. Darcy finally even tells her about Wickham's shameful actions in the past. And in the end she realizes her error and comes to love him greatly, becoming a very happy *Mrs.* Darcy.

Are you more like Elizabeth, quick to judge and easy to anger, or more like Mr. Darcy, patiently holding your tongue, even when things seem unfair? Just think about how long-suffering the Lord is with us. In 2 Peter 1:5–7, we are given a list of things to cultivate in ourselves: "Giving all diligence, add to your faith virtue, to virtue knowledge, to knowledge self-control, to self-control perseverance, to perseverance godliness, to godliness brotherly kindness, and to brotherly kindness love."

Self-control and perseverance—patience, in other words—lead to love, and that is the primary thing that Christians are supposed to exemplify. The next time you find yourself being an Elizabeth Bennett, instead take Mr. Darcy's route.

## A PRAYER

Dear God, patience is not something I enjoy cultivating, but I know I can do it with Your guidance. Please help me show my love for others through patience. Amen.

## TAKE ACTION

- Is there something on your heart that you hope for, but have doubts it will happen? Begin praying for it today, and prepare yourself to be patient, keeping that person or situation in your prayers, for years if necessary.
- Write down 2 Peter 1:5–7 on an index card and read it several times this week. Look for opportunities to exercise these qualities.

# 32

# Bravery

Dorothy, *The Wizard of Oz*

*Though an army besiege me, my heart will not fear.*

—Psalm 27:3 NIV

If you asked most people who the bravest character was in *The Wizard of Oz*, their first impulse might be to name the Cowardly Lion. It was he, after all, who famously found his roar. But actually, it was young Dorothy Gale who was the real hero of the story as she repeatedly faced down evil beings all throughout the movie.

One of the very first scenes of MGM's classic film finds Dorothy bravely defending her little dog, Toto, against the evil Miss Elvira Gulch. Gulch had come to take Toto away for biting her. "Oh, no, no! I won't let you take him!" Dorothy cries. "You go away, or I'll bite you myself! . . . You wicked old witch! Uncle Henry, Auntie Em, don't let 'em take Toto! Don't let her take him—please!" Miss Gulch absconds with the pup, but he escapes her clutches and runs back home.

*The Wizard of Oz* showprint, created and copyright, 1903 by the U.S. Lithograph Co., Russell-Morgan Print, Cincinnati and New York

Later, in Oz, Dorothy runs into the Wicked Witch of the West. The malevolent crone bears a striking resemblance to Miss Gulch, and she is just as evil. When the good witch Glinda warns Dorothy to get out of Oz as soon as she can, Dorothy once again steps out bravely, following the yellow brick road on a long journey to seek the Wizard of Oz's assistance in getting home.

Dorothy shows her bravery again when she and her new friends, the Scarecrow and the Tin Man, find themselves in a scary forest, nervously expecting to see "lions and tigers and bears." And when a lion does leap out at them and chases poor Toto, it is Dorothy who smacks him right on the nose.

Later Dorothy rescues Scarecrow when the evil witch tries to burn him up. Her heroic effort to douse him kills the Wicked Witch, who melts when splashed with some of the water.

Finally, Dorothy is the one who stands up to the Wizard when he tells them to come back the next day to talk to him about granting their wishes. They've delivered him the Wicked Witch's broom, as he'd demanded. Now he is putting them off when it is time to pay up on their deal. Dorothy shouts, "Tomorrow? Oh, but I want to go home *now* . . . If you were really great and powerful, you'd keep your promises!"

"Tomorrow? Oh, but I want to go home *now* . . . If you were really great and powerful, you'd keep your promises!"

**—DOROTHY, TO THE WIZARD**

Was Dorothy an invincible person? Of course not. She described herself as "Dorothy, the small and meek," when she first met the Wizard. And when captured and imprisoned by the Wicked Witch, she cried out, "I'm frightened. I'm frightened, Auntie Em."

Bravery is not the same as not being afraid. It's moving forward despite your fear. Many of the psalms were written when David was fearful. Armies chased him, and he rightfully feared for his life. But, he said, though an army besieged him, his heart would not fear (Ps. 27:3). Why?

> *For in the time of trouble*
> *He shall hide me in His pavilion;*
> *In the secret place of His tabernacle*
> *He shall hide me;*
> *He shall set me high upon a rock. (v. 5)*

We, too, can take heart and be brave because our Shepherd will never leave us. He will give us a strong heart and set our feet upon a rock.

## A PRAYER

Dear Father, sometimes, like Dorothy and like David, I feel besieged by the enemy. Thank You for giving me Your Word so I can know there is no need for my heart to fear. Amen.

## TAKE ACTION

- Take a month to read through and digest the psalms. They are full of hope and promise for anyone going through a fearful time and needing some "bravery armor."
- Memorize the most famous psalm, if you haven't already: Psalm 23. Then you will have it in your heart when you most need to be brave.
- If there's some challenge you face that makes you feel "small and meek," and you know you should conquer it, take one small step toward facing that fear.

# 33

# Eagerness

D'Artagnon, *The Three Musketeers*

> *Brethren, I do not count myself to have apprehended;*
> *but one thing I do, forgetting those things which*
> *are behind and reaching forward to those things*
> *which are ahead, I press toward the goal for the*
> *prize of the upward call of God in Christ Jesus.*
>
> **—Philippians 3:13–14**

It is just past eight in the morning one day when young d'Artagnon, a country boy with dreams of joining the Musketeers, arrives in Paris. So eager is he to use his sword that within minutes he has antagonized three Musketeers, who challenge him to duels that same day. When the four of them end up facing the guards of Cardinal Richelieu instead, he begs to be part of the fight: "I may not have the tunic, but I have the heart of a Musketeer!" The youngster, dashingly played by Michael York in the 1973 movie (perhaps, in my opinion, the best of the renditions of this famous story on the silver screen), shows his mettle that day, earning him the privilege of fighting beside the swashbuckling Athos, Porthos, and Aramis.

> "[I'm] gallant, courageous, discreet, active . . . loyal. You can trust me because I love you."
>
> **—D'ARTAGNON, TO CONSTANCE**

His eagerness shows itself again when he tries to convince the lovely Constance to let him be the one to carry an urgent missive to the Duke of Buckingham. The queen's life depends on its safe arrival, and he desperately wants Constance to entrust him with it. I'm "gallant, courageous, discreet, active . . . loyal. You can trust me because I love you." And indeed he does prove himself loyal to her and to her queen, winning her heart, the queen's favor, and his place as the fourth Musketeer.

When you think of your identity as a Christian, the first thing that may come to your mind might be "faithful" or "strong," and these things will certainly stand you in good stead throughout your life. But we are also called to be eager, like young d'Artagnon.

Paul encourages us in this way in his letter to the Philippians, where he urges them to press forward toward the goal for the prize of the upward call of God in Christ.

"Not that I have already attained, or am already perfected; but I press on, that I may lay hold of that for which Christ Jesus has also laid hold of me" (3:12).

We will all face disappointments, challenges, and tough situations, and these are the times we are most tempted to give up. That's just part of being human. But Paul tells us we are to put that aside and keep our eyes on Jesus, the author and finisher of our faith (Heb. 12:2). We aren't doing ourselves or anyone else a favor by allowing things to get us down and keep us from being effective in our Christian lives. Are you pressing eagerly toward the goal of Christ?

## A PRAYER

Dear Jesus, Paul tells us to press on toward the goal. Please be with me today as I strive eagerly toward the goal of being close to You, and protect me from distractions as I pursue You. Amen.

## TAKE ACTION

- Read Philippians 3:12–21 for the context of Paul's exhortation.
- Immerse yourself in the Word this week and press eagerly toward the goal.
- What have you been slacking off on or putting off until later? Attending youth group or Sunday

school? Asking your church how you can volunteer? Getting up early for your quiet time in the Word? Instead of pushing it to the end of your "To Do" list, try investing some prayer and energy into it and approach it with a sense of eagerness.

# 34
# Gallantry

Sir Lancelot, *First Knight*

> *Whoever desires to become great*
> *among you shall be your servant.*
>
> —Mark 10:43

If you were to ask folks for the most gallant fictional character they can name, many of them would probably say Sir Lancelot. He is, after all, famous for his gallantry, a trait defined by *Merriam-Webster's Collegiate Dictionary* as "an act of marked courtesy," "courteous attention to a lady," "amorous attention or pursuit," or "spirited and conspicuous bravery."

In the movie *First Knight*, Lancelot is the knight everyone aspires to be, adhering to the chivalric code that says that all knights should protect those who cannot protect themselves, as well as stay humble. Lancelot first displays his gallantry when he rescues Lady Guinevere from the clutches of her nemesis, Meleagant, a former knight of the Round Table who turned his back on King Arthur.

By saving her yet again from Meleagant—this time from his castle, where she's been imprisoned—Lancelot becomes one of Arthur's most beloved and trusted knights. And Guinevere becomes Arthur's wife.

Guinevere and Lancelot fall in love, but because he also loves Camelot and the king, Lancelot decides to walk away from the woman he loves. "I know what I must do now. I never believed in anything before. But I do believe in Camelot. I will serve it best by leaving. Tell the king that I will always remember that he saw the best in me."

The king discovers Guinevere and Lancelot sharing a good-bye kiss, which leads to their public trial for treason. Lancelot, again showing his gallantry, says, "My Lord, the queen is innocent. But if my life or my death serves Camelot, take it. Do what you like with me. Brother to brother, yours in life and death."

A final battle interrupts the trial, and Lancelot takes on Meleagant in an epic sword fight culminating in the evil knight's death. Unfortunately, King Arthur is also mortally wounded. The noble king gives his kingdom to Lancelot as he dies.

When you think of gallantry, do you think of the times when there were real kings and knights? Is chivalry really just a product of those times, or does it live on today?

Sadly, the answer may be that most believe chivalry is dead. A 2011 poll found that 76 percent of Americans believe our society is becoming more and more rude. We can each be a part of sending that poll back in the right direction by expressing ourselves civilly and honoring others. We can choose to hold the door open for the next person going through, or serve people in some other small way. And like the Knights of the Round Table, we can choose to stand up for others who are too weak to stand up for themselves. Psalm 82:3–4 tells us we should

> *Defend the poor and fatherless;*
> *Do justice to the afflicted and needy.*
> *Deliver the poor and needy;*
> *Free them from the hand of the wicked.*

If you're not doing so already, bring a little gallantry back into the world today.

## A PRAYER

Dear God, thank You for the gallant people I run into in my daily life. Help me also be someone who stands up for others and serves them. Amen.

## TAKE ACTION

- Keep your eye out for the next person who needs a little help, and step up. It may be as simple as helping someone with a heavy load or opening the supermarket door for a mom with a stroller, but it can make a big difference in that person's day.
- Read Psalm 149:1–4 to see how God feels about humble people.
- Check out a copy of William J. Bennett's *The Book of Virtues*, which will not only inspire you but also help you instill gallant hearts in other people in your life.

## 35

# Putting Others Before Yourself

Sydney Carton and Charles
Darnay, *A Tale of Two Cities*

> *God demonstrates His own love toward us, in that*
> *while we were still sinners, Christ died for us.*
>
> **—Romans 5:8**

It is the kind of love that can never be reconciled. Sydney
Carton knows he isn't good enough for the lovely Lucie
Manette. She doesn't return his feelings, although she
adores her friendship with the man. He swears to her, "It is
useless to say it I know but it rises out of my soul. For you
and for any dear to you I would do anything . . . I would
embrace any sacrifice for you and for those dear to you."
Little do either of them know that the French Revolution is
almost upon them, and that soon he will have the chance
to fulfill his vows in a way no one could have expected.

Lucie marries Charles Darnay, a good man who could have been Sydney Carton had Carton not made the choices he had in life. They even look alike, a fact that saves Darnay not once, but twice. The first time, Darnay was framed for treason and on trial for his life. His attorney undercuts the prosecution by having Darnay and fellow barrister Carton switch places. When the witness can't identify who is who, his testimony becomes worthless, and Darnay is found innocent.

"It is a far, far better thing that I do than I have ever done," Carton says, right before his turn at the guillotine. "It is a far, far better rest that I go to than I have ever known."

The second time has deadlier consequences. The peasants have stormed the Bastille in Paris and are executing all the "aristos" they can find in the city. Darnay, who is related to one of the worst of the aristocracy, but who has always supported the peasants, is captured and again put on trial. This time, simply because of who he is related to, he is found guilty and sentenced to the guillotine. How would he escape certain death?

It is that former wastrel and drunk, Sydney Carton, who, remembering his vow to Lucie, determines to swap places with Darnay and take his place in death. Through some clever scheming, Carton gets into the prison, drugs Darnay, and exchanges places with him in time to go to his death. "It is a far, far better thing that I do than I have ever done," he says right before his turn at the guillotine. "It is a far, far better rest that I go to than I have ever known."

As deeply, agonizingly, and desperately as Carton loved Lucie, that's only a shadow of how much our Father loves each of us, and He made the ultimate sacrifice because of it. He knew before you were even born that you would sin and He would need to save you. God sent Jesus not "to condemn the world, but to save the world through him. Whoever believes in him is not condemned, but whoever does not believe stands condemned already because they have not believed in the name of God's one and only Son" (John 3:17–18 NIV).

Sometimes in the business of our daily lives, we forget the impact of those words. We are not condemned, because God sent His Son to die in our place. Each of us bears a heavy responsibility because of this unwarranted gift. We are to look for ways to be like Christ, like Sydney Carton, and lay down our lives for others. Do you live in a self-sacrificial way, putting others before yourself?

## A PRAYER

Thank You, God, for your Son's sacrifice He made for me and everyone in my life. Help me remember how much You love me, and help me to put others first. Amen.

# TAKE ACTION

- Watch the film *The Passion of the Christ*, to help bring home exactly what Christ suffered for us.
- One organization that continually puts others before itself is the Red Cross. Check out their website, www.redcross.org, to see how you can donate blood, money, or time.

# 36
# Teachability

Eliza Doolittle, *My Fair Lady*

*Show me Your ways, LORD;*
*Teach me Your paths.*
*Lead me in Your truth and teach me,*
*For You are the God of my salvation:*
*On You I wait all the day.*

—Psalm 25:4–5

One wet evening in 1912 London, a poor flower girl with a heavy Cockney accent meets someone who will change her life forever. His name is Professor Henry Higgins (famously played by Rex Harrison in the film *My Fair Lady*), and he has some strong feelings about the English language. Her name is Eliza Doolittle (played by a plucky Audrey Hepburn). Professor Higgins, a language expert, makes the offhanded comment to his friend Colonel Pickering that he can teach the girl to speak properly so she might get a job working at a real flower shop. The next day he finds Eliza on his doorstep, demanding lessons:

"I want to be a lady in a flow'r shop 'stead of sellin' at the corner of Tottenham Court Road. But they won't take me unless I can talk more genteel. He said 'e could teach me. Well, 'ere I am ready to pay 'im."

> "I want to be a lady in a flow'r shop 'stead of sellin' at the corner of Tottenham Court Road. But they won't take me unless I can talk more genteel."
>
> —ELIZA DOOLITTLE

What follows is a bet between the two gentlemen that Higgins can train Eliza in elocution and present her at the Embassy Ball in six months. The deal is struck, and Miss Doolittle is on her way to some trying months as she works night after night into the wee hours of the morning to master the English language. It seems she'll never be able to properly pronounce "In Hartford, Herriford, and Hampshire, hurricanes hardly ever happen." And "The rain in Spain stays mainly in the plain." Not to mention "How *kind* of you to let me come." She perseveres, though, conquers the lovely English accent, and the ball is a triumph. Eliza even dances with a prince. She has become a lovely, articulate lady.

None of this would have been possible if Eliza had not approached the professor with determination and a willingness to learn. No one is teachable who thinks he or she has all the answers already. It requires an openness to admit you can learn from others.

Jesus is called Teacher many times in the Bible, and He left us His Word so we can continue to learn from Him as He leads us in truth. Look at these interesting facts:

1. Christ was called *teacher* 45 times, but was never called *preacher* once.
2. The terms equivalent to *teacher* that refer to Christ total 61.
3. The term *Master* is used 66 times in the King James Bible, and 54 of these come from a Greek word meaning "teacher" or "schoolmaster."
4. Christ is referred to 45 times as teaching and 11 times as preaching.
5. He was recognized as a great teacher—not as a ruler, politician, miracle worker, or a mover and shaker among men.
6. Often His teaching was coupled with His preaching. (See Matt. 4:23)

Are you open to learning from the greatest Teacher who ever lived?

## A PRAYER

Dear Lord, sometimes I close myself off to learning from others because I think I know best. Please grant me the discernment to know when I need to open myself to further teaching. Amen.

# TAKE ACTION

- If you desire wisdom, there is no better place to find it than Proverbs. Start with Proverbs 1–10, and see if it doesn't make you thirsty for more of the wisdom of the Bible.
- Have you considered a one-year plan to read through the Bible? Determine that this will be the year to follow through. You'll be amazed at what you'll learn, and even more amazed at how your relationship with God grows.
- Do you have an expertise that you can share with another person? It may be something small, but that person may appreciate more than you'll ever know that you took the time to teach him or her.

# 37

# Forgiveness

Esmeralda, *The Hunchback of Notre Dame*

> *"And whenever you stand praying, if you*
> *have anything against anyone, forgive*
> *him, that your Father in heaven may*
> *also forgive you your trespasses."*

—Mark 11:25

It takes a real hero to forgive someone who's done an evil deed against him. In 1939's *The Hunchback of Notre Dame,* the hero is an unlikely person, a young gypsy girl named Esmeralda (played by the lovely Maureen O'Hara).

It had been decreed that no gypsies were to be allowed in the town, and so she flees into the cathedral of Notre Dame for sanctuary. There she encounters the vile Frollo, who takes her to the resident bell ringer, a hunchbacked man named Quasimodo. When Esmeralda flees at the terrifying sight of Quasimodo, Frollo orders him to chase her down, which he does. Fortunately she is rescued by

Captain Phoebus, who is enamored of her and wants to protect her. Quasimodo is punished for the crime of abduction: fifty lashes and an hour on the pillory—a platform where he is tied up for public display after his beating. Here Esmeralda models for us what true forgiveness looks like.

> When Esmeralda is convicted of a murder she did not commit, it looks as if there is nowhere but the gallows for her.

"Water, water," Quasimodo begs the crowd. The derisive mob is silenced when Esmeralda—the girl he has terrified and chased just the night before—is the one who has mercy on him and gives him the drink he so badly craves. She doesn't know it yet, but that action will be the very thing that saves her life later.

When Esmeralda is convicted of a murder she did not commit, it looks as if there is nowhere but the gallows for her. The noose is right in front of her face when the hunchback swings down on a rope, scoops her up, and carries her back to the safety of Notre Dame. There he confesses to her that he saved her because she had brought him water.

Like Quasimodo, we, too, have been offered forgiveness and the water of life. We can drink deeply at the well of Jesus' love, and know our sins are washed away. Remember, too, that we are required by our Savior to forgive others as we ourselves have been forgiven. And it makes Him sad when we have a spirit of unforgiveness. Consider the following consequences of unforgiveness:

1. You'll be tormented by Satan—you give Satan a foothold to enter your life and mess with what you value the most (Eph. 4:26–27).
2. You won't be able to pray (Mark 11:26; 1 Peter 3:7).
3. You'll be plagued with guilt (Matt. 6:14–15).
4. You'll be controlled by the person you are unwilling to forgive.

Forgiving does not mean that what others have done to us is okay, or that we'll forget that it happened. It does not mean they have apologized or tried to make amends. It simply means we hand our anger and hatred over to God and let Him handle the wrong. It frees us from bondage to our own emotions and allows us to move on with life in a healthier way.

Who can you forgive today?

## A PRAYER

Dear Lord, forgiveness is something that does not come easily to me. Please help me discern where in my life I need to forgive, and help me hand that over to You. Amen.

## TAKE ACTION

- Grab a sheet of paper and write down the names of people you have been holding a grudge against. Pray in earnest about forgiving these people, even if they have not apologized to you.
- Are you in need of forgiveness from someone? If you can't bring yourself to apologize in person, try writing a letter to the individual you have wronged.

# 38
# Honesty

Sheriff Andy Taylor, *The Andy Griffith Show*

> *Therefore, whatever you want men to do to you, do
> also to them, for this is the Law and the Prophets.*

—Matthew 7:12

One of our most beloved hometown heroes is Sheriff Andy
Taylor, from *The Andy Griffith Show*. He offered the best of
folk wisdom, practical know-how, and small-town values,
like patriotism, faith, and honesty. But even heroes have to
learn things the hard way sometimes, as Andy did in the
episode titled "The Horse Trader."

As Andy is at the office one day, Opie meets him at
the door and announces he'll have some roller skates soon.
When pressed by Andy, he explains that he'll be trading
some "licorice seeds" to his friend Jerry in return for a pair
of skates. Opie had been swindled himself when he traded
away his new cap gun to Tommy for the seeds, which pre-
dictably did not grow licorice sticks. Andy reminds Opie of
an important truth.

"You know that you've been taught the Golden Rule, do unto others as you would have them do unto you?" he queries Opie.

"Yes, Pa."

"You think you've been following that rule?"

"Sure," replies Opie. "Tommy did it unto me, and now I'm doing it unto Jerry."

"Uh, I believe you're bendin' that rule just a little bit. Now, the Golden Rule says that you're supposed to be honest and square dealin' with other folks. Now, tellin' your friends that them seeds is going to grow licorice sticks is kinda far away from what you'd call square dealin', and it's awful close to what you'd call cheatin' . . . And I know that you wouldn't feel good cheatin' your friend. Now, I'll tell you what to do. You just keep them licorice seeds and forget this whole trade until you got something to dicker with, all right? Now, just always remember, honesty is the best policy."

> "Now, the Golden Rule says that you're supposed to be honest and square dealin' with other folks."
>
> **—SHERIFF ANDY TAYLOR**

Opie doesn't think honesty is so great, since he ended up with no cap gun or roller skates, but he obeys his dad.

Soon Andy's own words come back to haunt him when Ralph Mason, an antique dealer, comes through town. The town council has tasked Andy to sell the town's old cannon that is in rough shape, and Mason is just the guy to buy it. Andy talks up the cannon by stretching the truth: "That crack right there come from a direct hit while Teddy Roosevelt was draggin' her up San Juan Hill. When he yelled 'Charge!' this is what he charged with . . . See the initials right there, T. R. Teddy Roosevelt." Barney and Opie are both witnesses to this conversation and try to correct Andy, but Andy shoos them away and makes the sale for $175.

Later Opie rolls up to Andy on his new skates. He'd taken his father's lesson to heart and traded a broken cuff link for them. He'd told his friend the cuff link was a button off the uniform of General George Washington.

"You've just broken the Golden Rule . . . and cheated," Andy scolds Opie.

But Opie comes back with "I think we both broke the Golden Rule." Andy hems and haws, but finally he has to admit the rules are the same for kids and adults.

"I think you're right, Opie. I'll tell you what. Now, you take them skates back to Jerry, and I got a little fence mendin' to do of my own, all right?"

Andy is true to his word and tells Mason, "The deal we made is based on lies . . . Everything I told you about Teddy Roosevelt and San Juan Hill and all like that, well, I made that up, and I have to be honest with you."

Mason appreciates Andy's honesty, and he buys the cannon for $20, a win for the town, Mr. Mason, and the Golden Rule.

It would be better if we could be honest with each other in the first place. Most of the world's problems could be solved pretty quickly if we were.

In Scripture we see a story of the ultimate punishment for those who would lie. It is the story of Ananias and his wife, Sapphira, who sold their property to distribute among all the Christians in Jerusalem. They had good intentions, but they made a mistake: when they gave their earnings to the apostles, they told them they were giving everything, but they secretly held back some portion of their earnings. Ananias paid a heavy price for that lie.

"Why have you conceived this thing in your heart?" asked Peter. "You have not lied to men but to God."

Upon hearing the words, Ananias fell over and died. Young men scooped him up, took him outside, and buried him (Acts 5:4–6). Awhile later, Sapphira came to the apostles, not realizing what had happened to her husband, and she, too, lied. *Zap.* She fell over dead as well. God does not appreciate being lied to.

Are you honest in all your dealings, or do you occasionally tell a small untruth? God knows what is in your heart, so live a life of freedom by avoiding this sin.

## A PRAYER

Dear Jesus, help me to be a good example of honesty to others, and help me to remember that even in the small things, You see what is in my heart. Amen.

## TAKE ACTION

- If you have been dishonest with someone, now is the time to correct that. Take a step toward coming clean.
- If someone asks you for your "honest opinion" about something he is engaged in, don't just tell him something you think he wants to hear. That is a form of dishonesty and does the other person no good. Instead, tailor your comments constructively, focusing on how he can improve, or give him a sincere compliment if there is no improvement needed.
- Have you been dishonest with yourself? It's easy to fool yourself into taking certain actions when you really want to do something, but check yourself and align your desires with God's Word. Do they match?

# 39
# Optimism

Don Quixote, *Man of La Mancha*

> *Beloved, we are confident of better things concerning*
> *you, yes, things that accompany salvation . . . For*
> *God is not unjust to forget your work and labor of*
> *love which you have shown toward His name, in that*
> *you have ministered to the saints, and do minister.*

—Hebrews 6:9–10

Have you heard the word *quixotic*? It means "foolishly impractical, especially in the pursuit of ideals; *especially*: marked by rash lofty romantic ideas or extravagantly chivalrous action," and the word found its way into our language because of the author Miguel de Cervantes.

In the early 1600s the Spaniard wrote of a hero named Don Quixote who becomes famous for some strange acts of chivalry. Quixote's real name is Alonso Quijana, a country gent who becomes fascinated by books about the evil in this world and ponders how to make it a better one. And he reads about knights in shining armor and their code of chivalry. Finally he "lays down the melancholy burden of sanity" and decides to become a knight errant "and sally forth to roam the world in search of adventures, to right all wrongs, to mount a crusade, to raise up the weak and those in need." He becomes Don Quixote de La Mancha.

Along with his trusty squire, Sancho Panza, Quixote rides the countryside, tilting at windmills that he believes are horrible beasts and battling muleteers for the honor of his lady, Dulcinea, who is just a scullery maid. His horse, a skinny specimen, becomes his fine steed, Rocinante.

> "I come in a world of iron to make a world of gold."
> —DON QUIXOTE DE LA MANCHA

Throughout the movie, *The Man of La Mancha*, Quixote maintains his sense of optimism. Whatever is wrong, he imagines he rights it. Whatever is dirty he imagines is pristine. Dulcinea asks of his crazy acts, "Why do you do these things?" He replies, "I come in a world of iron to make a world of gold." Cervantes, himself a character in the movie, says, "It is true I am guilty of these charges: an idealist. But I have never had the courage to believe in nothing."

Are you an idealist like Cervantes? Always looking for the good in everything and everyone? Optimistically you hope for the best outcome to every situation, sometimes against all odds. Some people may look down on you for this, but it is a special gift. While we all look to a better world, we are called to love each other today, and what better way to love others than to believe in them? Christ looks at each of us sinners and sees a beloved child. He looks at our fallen world and proclaims it will be new again. And He made you just the way you are: someone who sees beauty and brings it to others.

Perhaps you tend to be more of a glass-half-empty person. In that case, remember this promise of Paul's: "And we know that all things work together for good to those who love God, to those who are the called according to His purpose" (Rom. 8:28). These words remind us that even if disaster befalls us, we have reason to rejoice. No matter what the situation, the Creator of the universe will work it for our good. That alone is reason for celebration and optimism.

## A PRAYER

Dear Jesus, thank You for the optimists in my life. Please help me to appreciate that personality trait for the gift that it is and to cultivate it in my own personality. Amen.

## TAKE ACTION

- Make a list of three things you can make better through your actions. It's surprising how much you can influence people and situations, even in a small way.

- Today, see how many people you can smile at. You can bring optimism to people in such a simple way.
- If you have small children in your life, make a "joy" card with them, a drawing of something that makes them happy.

# 40

# Responsibility

## Spider-Man

*Let us draw near with a true heart in full assurance of faith, having our hearts sprinkled from an evil conscience and our bodies washed with pure water.*

—Hebrews 10:22

Peter Parker's beloved uncle lay dying on the pavement. Just hours earlier Uncle Ben had tried to tell Peter something important, a bit of wisdom from an older generation. But Peter, being a young man, didn't have the maturity to accept it. He had rebuffed Ben then, and now he'd never have the chance to apologize.

How did he get to this terrible place? Talking about a fight Peter had gotten into with the school bully, Uncle Ben had said, "Peter, these are the years when a man changes into the man he's gonna be the rest of his life. Just be careful who you change into. This guy Flash Thompson, he probably deserved what happened. But just because you can beat him up doesn't give you the right to. Remember, with great power comes great responsibility."

Peter had just developed his spider-powers of strength and great dexterity and was learning to use them, but he wasn't using the best of judgment yet when it came to responsibility. When one thief robbed another thief, he let the second one escape, figuring the first thief deserved it. But he learned what can happen when he didn't use the responsibility of his powers well: the thief ended up carjacking and murdering Uncle Ben just minutes later.

What is your responsibility as a Christian? Many things, including loving others and caring for the poor around you. But before any of that, you are called to personal responsibility for your faith. We are all expected to have faith in all things and know that no person or set of circumstances can come between us and our Savior.

"We should never blame our spiritual failures on others."

—A. W. TOZER

Theologian A. W. Tozer said that "we should never blame our spiritual failures on others. The habit of seeking weak consolation by blaming our poor showing on unfavorable circumstances is a damaging evil and should not for one moment be tolerated. To live a lifetime believing that our inner weakness is the result of an external situation and then find at the last that we ourselves were to blame—that is too painful to be contemplated."

Tozer continues by reminding us that we should let our souls take "a quiet attitude of faith and love toward God, and from there on the responsibility is God's. He will make good on His commitments. There is not on earth a lonely spot where a Christian cannot live and be spiritually victorious if God sends him there. He carries his own climate with him or has it supplied supernaturally when he arrives."

Knowing that God will meet us in any circumstance in which we find ourselves, step forward with confidence and be victorious. Do you take responsibility for your own faith?

## A PRAYER

Dear Lord, I sometimes let other people or difficult circumstances come between me and You. I know I can't blame anyone else for this. Please forgive me and strengthen my faith. Amen.

## TAKE ACTION

- Check your attitude. Are you doing what Tozer said and allowing other people or circumstances into your spiritual thinking? Don't let anyone else come between you and God.
- Understand that your responsibility is to have an attitude of faith; God will supply what you need to be spiritually victorious.

# 41

# Relentlessness

Marlin, Nemo's Dad, *Finding Nemo*

*And let us not grow weary while doing good, for in*
*due season we shall reap if we do not lose heart.*

—Galatians 6:9

The blue marlin fish is one of the biggest fish in the oceans, reaching fourteen feet long and weighing more than 1,985 pounds. You can recognize a marlin by its prominent dorsal fin and vicious-looking, spiked upper jaw. Marlins are among the favorite sport fish because of their size and the fight they put up when they find themselves on the hook.

In *Finding Nemo*, we meet a little clown fish named Marlin. Upon first seeing him, you might think he has nothing in common with his namesake, but that's not the case at all. In fact, when his son, Nemo, is snatched by a diver and taken to Australia, you see a marlin-sized determination to fight for his son's life. His journey takes him through a party of sharks and the deadly jellyfish forest, and finds him swept up in the East Australian Current with a school of sea turtles. At one point three sea birds gossip about him:

> **MALE BIRD 1:** I mean, it sounds like this guy's gonna stop at—
> **MALE BIRD 2:**—nothing until he finds his son. I sure hope he makes it.
> **MALE BIRD 3:** That's one dedicated father, if you ask me.

Marlin arrives where Nemo is being held just in time to see what he believes is his son's body. Grief-stricken, he swims dejectedly off to the fishing grounds, not realizing his son is still alive. Thankfully, Marlin's friend Dory finds Nemo and brings him to Marlin, and they have a joyful reunion after one more challenging obstacle.

Marlin's quest had seemed hopeless. He had stopped at nothing to get to his son, only to be seemingly too late. Like Marlin, sometimes we pursue a goal, only to give up just before we would have seen success. God will let you know if it's time to stop striving toward something you've been relentlessly working toward for a long time. He desires our success on things he's blessed, and we need to remember to keep praying all the way through.

> "That's one dedicated father, if you ask me."

Ephesians 3:20 reminds us that God "is able to do exceedingly abundantly above all that we ask or think, according to the power that works in us." The power of this scripture rests in our being wise enough to ask God for our needs while living through His power. Remember that you're not alone if you're on a quest for something that is difficult; you have a power that works in you from God Himself.

## A PRAYER

Dear God, sometimes things get so hard I just want to quit. Please help me continue on if it's something I know You've blessed. Help me to remember to ask You for help and to live through Your power working in me. Amen.

## TAKE ACTION

- Memorize Proverbs 19:21: "There are many plans in a man's heart, nevertheless the LORD's counsel—that will stand."
- Are you about to give up on something you've been working toward? Take heart and know that if your plans are from God, He is able to do "exceedingly abundantly" above all you ask.

# 42

# Resourcefulness

Mick Dundee, *"Crocodile" Dundee*

> *Those who built on the wall, and those who*
> *carried burdens, loaded themselves so that with*
> *one hand they worked at construction, and with*
> *the other held a weapon. Every one of the builders*
> *had his sword girded at his side as he built.*

—Nehemiah 4:17–18

In *"Crocodile" Dundee*, it's hard to tell who is wilier, the crocs or the fellow who poaches them, Mick Dundee. Before traveling to Australia's Walkabout Creek to meet Dundee, New York journalist Sue Charlton thought she'd seen it all. But Dundee is something else entirely. He uses all his resources to impress her, including calming a water buffalo with a mystical hand signal. He also dances with the Aborigines in one of their ceremonies and, at one point, kills a snake with his bare hands. He even provides Sue with an outback feast gathered from the brush,

Paul Hogan in *"Crocodile" Dundee II*, directed by John Cornell (Paramount, 1988)

impressing her with his resourcefulness. In short, he uses every means at his disposal to win the girl, and in the end she falls for him!

In the Old Testament book of Nehemiah, we find another resourceful man, although his goal was much loftier and worthier than that of Mick Dundee. His name was Nehemiah, and he lived in the period after the Babylonian captivity when the Israelites came back to Jerusalem. Since its fall, the burned-out city had been without walls, just a hulk of what it had once been. Nehemiah was a cupbearer for Persian king Artaxerxes and asked for the ruler's help as Nehemiah mustered his resources to go back to Jerusalem to rebuild its walls:

> "If it pleases the king, let letters be given to me for the governors of the region beyond the River, that they must permit me to pass through till I come to Judah, and a letter to Asaph the keeper of the king's forest, that he must give me timber to make beams for the gates of the citadel which pertains to the temple, for the city wall, and for the house that I will occupy." And the king granted them to me according to the good hand of my God upon me. (Neh. 2:7–8)

Without a wall to protect them, Nehemiah and his men had to defend the city at the same time they were trying do a huge construction job. After they gathered their lumber, they still had to build it without a neighborhood Lowe's or Home Depot. Scripture tells us they had to build with one hand and hold their weapons with the other. Imagine building under those circumstances! One man mocked them: "What are these feeble Jews doing? Will they fortify themselves? Will they offer sacrifices? Will they complete [the city wall] in a day? Will they revive the stones from the heaps of rubbish—stones that are burned?" (Neh. 4:2). But God had called Nehemiah to be resourceful, and in spite of the odds against the cupbearer and his building crew, together they got the job done.

We, too, are called to be resourceful with what God has given us. When you feel you are called to do something, don't think about all the reasons you can't, even if there are some real logistical difficulties. Instead emulate Nehemiah, who mustered his resources from nothing and rebuilt the wall around Jerusalem. God will provide you the means to complete what you start in His name.

## A PRAYER

Lord, thank You for the resources You give me when You call me into Your service. Help me always remember that You will provide for my needs. Amen.

# TAKE ACTION

- Read the book of Nehemiah this week to find out the rest of the story about the wall and the Israelites.
- If you desire to be a resource to others, check out Habitat for Humanity and help build something yourself!

# 43
# Faithfulness

Nathaniel, *The Last of the Mohicans*

> *I am persuaded that neither death nor life, nor angels*
> *nor principalities nor powers, nor things present*
> *nor things to come, nor height nor depth, nor any*
> *other created thing, shall be able to separate us from*
> *the love of God which is in Christ Jesus our Lord.*

—Romans 8:38–39

The roaring waterfall pounds outside their cave as the small group huddles there in hiding. Cora can hear her beloved Nathaniel having a heated discussion with his Mohican friends, and she knows what they are talking about. If Nathaniel and his friends abandon them now, there is hope that they can save the rest of the group later. If they stay, all of them—including British officer Major Duncan Heyward and Cora's sister, Alice—will be slaughtered right there by the Indians who pursue them.

"I want you to go!" Cora urges Nathaniel.

"If we go there's a chance there won't be a fight," he explains. "There's no [gun]powder. If we don't go there's no chance, none! You understand?"

Cora is giving up. "You've done everything you can do. Save yourself! If the worst happens, if only one of us survives, something of the other does too."

But he insists, "No. You stay alive. If they don't kill you they'll take you north up to Huron land. You're strong; you survive. You stay alive, no matter what occurs. I will find you. No matter how long it takes, no matter how far. I will find you."

As Nathaniel and his friends jump out into the raging river, leaving the rest of the group to the approaching Indians, Cora is terrified. But true to his word, he tracks down the captives through mountainous terrain and forests. After finding them in a Huron camp, he offers his life for those of the captives and talks the chief into sparing some of them. The chief decides that Cora will be burned alive. But it is Major Heyward whom the Huron end up burning at the stake, instead of Cora, bravely leaving Nathaniel to take care of Cora from then on.

> "No matter how long it takes, no matter how far. I will find you."
>
> **—NATHANIEL, TO CORA**

All of us have had moments in our lives when, like Cora under the waterfall, we've felt left on our own with no one to help, no one to back us up. We reach for our Bibles, and we pray, but it feels like there's no one there to answer our prayers. In these times we must remember that God knew what we would need today before we woke up. He is right there, and His footsteps go before ours in any situation. He is there for our small needs and our great ones. Recall the comforting hymn "Great Is Thy Faithfulness":

*Great is Thy faithfulness, O God my Father,*
*There is no shadow of turning with Thee:*
*Thou changest not, Thy compassions, they fail not,*
*As Thou hast been, Thou forever wilt be.*
*Great is Thy faithfulness! Great is Thy faithfulness!*
*Morning by morning new mercies I see;*
*All I have needed Thy hand hath provided,*
*Great is Thy faithfulness, Lord, unto me!*

Indeed, all we need, His hand has already provided.

## A PRAYER

Dear Father, it is You we turn to when we feel everyone else has failed us. I know in times of distress I must remember that You are more faithful than any person could be, and that You know my needs before I even pray to You. Amen.

## TAKE ACTION

- Write down three areas in which you are grateful that God's been faithful to you. Pray a prayer of thanksgiving for these.
- Read Psalm 37 and memorize the verses about feeding on God's faithfulness, verses 1–4.

# 44
# Duty

Horatio Hornblower, *Captain Horatio Hornblower*

> *"So you also, when you have done all that you*
> *were commanded, say, 'We are unworthy servants;*
> *we have only done what was our duty.'"*
>
> —Luke 17:10 ESV

For English Royal Navy captain Horatio Hornblower, a sense of duty was central to his character. When everything else in this time of war was in confusion, he could fall back on it. He would have need of it as the captain of the HMS *Lydia*, a thirty-six-gun frigate, which had orders to sail on a secret mission. Captain Hornblower was to provide arms to "El Supremo," a leader in Central America, so that he could rebel against Spain, which was at war with Britain at that time, the era of the Napoleonic Wars.

They have been at sea for seven months, and the crew is cranky to the point of being semi-mutinous. They don't know where they are going, the food and water are being rationed, and they are dropping like flies from scurvy. But Hornblower, knowing his duty is to complete the mission, refuses to turn for land and continues on toward the goal. He writes in his log:

> Thursday—I told them [the crew] we were within one hundred miles of our destination. I told them this only to keep hope alive. But pray God that my calculations were correct. It must come or we will surely die.

Fortunately, they reach Central America the next day, and the mission is accomplished.

Later in the war, his personal sense of duty is manifest when he, his friend Mr. Bush, and seaman Quist are captured by the French and on a carriage ride to Paris, where they are to be tried for piracy. They and their crew had sunk four French ships of the line. Mr. Bush's leg was injured in the battle.

"It's all or none of us."

**—CAPTAIN HORNBLOWER**

"How is it now, Bush?" Hornblower asks his friend as they all bump along in the carriage.

"It's not my leg that's worrying me, sir. It's knowing you won't even try to make a break as long as I'm here," answers Bush.

"I'm afraid he's delirious, Quist."

Quist replies, "He's not, sir. He's talking sense. If you get a chance, why don't you have a go, sir? I'll stick with Mr. Bush."

"It's all or none of us," Hornblower asserts.

In a daring move, they do manage to escape—together—and in a series of adventures, make it back to England in triumph.

Captain Hornblower had a clear sense of his military and personal duties. Do you know what your duties are as a Christian? Is it to go to church each Sunday? Perhaps it's to raise your children in the faith? Is it to love others? The answer is *yes* to all of these, and much more. Simply, Jesus bought us with His supreme sacrifice. This makes us His bondservants. Luke 17:10 tells us, "We are unworthy servants; we have only done what was our duty" (ESV). And what are we called to do? In Paul's letter to the Ephesians, he says:

> I, therefore, the prisoner of the Lord, beseech you to walk worthy of the calling with which you were called, with all lowliness and gentleness, with longsuffering, bearing with one another in love, endeavoring to keep the unity of the Spirit in the bond of peace. (4:1–3)

Christianity is an honorable calling that requires our entire lives, not just little bits of it here and there, and that brings with it a certain sense of duty. We are to be gentle and long-suffering, bearing with one another in love. Like Hornblower's, our code of behavior should be incorporated into our character so we can fall back on it in times of trouble. When in doubt, remember you are a bondservant, and your ultimate goal is to bring glory to Christ.

## A PRAYER

Dear Lord, thank you for paying the ultimate price for me. Help me to remember that I'm Your grateful bondservant and to do everything to Your glory. Amen.

## TAKE ACTION

- Read and memorize Ephesians 4:1–3, and learn what Paul considered our duty as Christ followers.
- List three ways you can "keep the unity of the Spirit in the bond of peace." Apply it to your family life, work world, school, or church activities.
- What do you think it means to be a bondservant? Go to BibleGateway.com and type the word *bondservant* in the search box to see all the Bible has to say about this important word.

# 45
# Community

The Magnificent Seven

*As each one has received a gift, minister*
*it to one another, as good stewards*
*of the manifold grace of God.*

—1 Peter 4:10

It's not often a film has such a star-studded cast, and that's
one reason *The Magnificent Seven* is still one of the most
popular Westerns. Based on the Japanese classic *Seven
Samurai* and released in 1960, it boasted the talents of Yul
Brynner, Steve McQueen, Eli Wallach, Robert Vaughn,
Charles Bronson, and James Coburn, among others.

In the movie, a group of Mexican villagers hires Chris
Adams (Yul Brynner) to come to their town to rid them of
Calvera, a bandit who, with a small army of men, periodi-
cally raids their village, steals everything for which they've
worked so hard, and harasses their women. Chris knows,
however, that dispatching the marauders is more than a

Yul Brynner and Steve McQueen in *The Magnificent Seven*, directed by John Sturges (United Artists, 1960)

one-man job, so he signs on six more men. Separate, they are trouble—just gunfighters and gamblers and drifters—but together they form an intimidating force.

This disparate group comes together for a single purpose: to fight a number many times their size. Once they arrive in the village, a curious thing happens: the villagers win them over with their generosity and earnestness. One of the seven falls in love with a local girl, another is adopted by a group of children as their hero, and still another ponders giving up his life as a gunfighter to settle down there and farm. They teach the town's men to shoot, and they build a wall together. The "job" starts to be more than just a job.

By the time the banditos descend on the town again, the Seven and the villagers have formed a solidarity that proves impossible to beat. Although they far outnumber their opponents, Calvera and his men are defeated, and the town is free of their terror forever.

It's amazing how when we come together, what we can accomplish increases manyfold. Jesus tells us, "I say to you that if two of you agree on earth concerning anything that they ask, it will be done for them by My Father in heaven. For where two or three are gathered together in My name, I am there in the midst of them" (Matt. 18:19–20).

God's authority and power are present whenever two or three of His disciples are gathered together. Whatever you do as part of your personal worship, be sure it includes some time with other believers. It can be as simple as asking

> We're meant to gather together to share God's Word and our lives.

a friend to pray with you, having a Bible study with your kids or friends, joining a small group at your church, or attending weekly services. If you're married, set aside time to pray with your spouse. We're meant to gather together to share God's Word and our lives. As long as we're praying God's will, together we form a solidarity that's impossible to beat.

## A PRAYER

Father, thank You for other believers I can share my life with. Help me to make spending time with them a part of my daily life. Amen.

## TAKE ACTION

- Choose a Bible study from your local bookstore and invite a few friends to go through it with you.
- Look into your church's small group program or youth group and consider if that's a good way for you to plug in with other people.
- Help organize a committee to secure funding to build a playground in an underprivileged neighborhood in your town.

# 46
# Faith in God

## Judah Ben-Hur, *Ben-Hur*

> *I, a prisoner in the Lord, encourage you to live the
> kind of life which proves that God has called you. Be
> humble and gentle in every way. Be patient with
> each other and lovingly accept each other. Through
> the peace that ties you together, do your best
> to maintain the unity that the Spirit gives.*
>
> —Ephesians 4:1–3 GW

*Thrum, thrum, thrum, thrum.* The rhythmic pounding of
the galley master's drum keeps a deadly beat for the rowers.
In the bowels of the Roman ship, rows of slaves keep the
vessel moving as they serve out the remaining days of their
lives. Most would live less than a year in the inhumane con-
ditions. One, however, is starting his fourth year as a galley
slave. Known simply as "Number 41," he doesn't have the
air of subservience or desperation that the others do.

Summoned to Roman consul Quintus Arrius's cabin,

Number 41, named Judah Ben-Hur, stands with a sense of purpose as Arrius offers him a ray of hope: Would he work for the consul as a charioteer back in Rome? To the consul's surprise, the slave turns him down. Ben-Hur's burning desire is to escape and get vengeance on Messala, a childhood friend-turned-enemy, for wrongfully imprisoning him and his mother and sister and delivering him into slavery.

"What do you think will save you?" Arrius asks Ben-Hur.

"The God of my fathers."

"Your God has forsaken you. He has no more power than the images I pray to. Your God will not help you."

> "It's a strange, stubborn faith you keep," observes the consul. "To believe that existence has a purpose. A sane man would have learned to lose it long before this."

But Ben-Hur has faith: "I will not be here forever . . . I cannot believe that God has let me live these three years to die chained to an oar."

"It's a strange, stubborn faith you keep," observes the consul. "To believe that existence has a purpose. A sane man would have learned to lose it long before this . . . Go back to your oar, 41."

But when the ship goes into battle and the other slaves are chained to their benches, Number 41 is not. By order of the consul, he is left loose so he'll have a fighting chance if the ship sinks—a bit of grace in the midst of misery. The consul's mercy pays off when Ben-Hur saves his life during the naval battle. Arrius takes Ben-Hur to Rome and adopts him as his son.

The newly freed man meets his nemesis, Messala, on the chariot track, each of them leading a team of beautiful horses. As Ben-Hur prepares to race his enemy, the desire for revenge sears his heart still. "God forgive me for seeking vengeance, but my path is set. Into your hands I commit my life. Do with me as you will." Despite his faith, the sin of hatred still keeps hold of his soul, even after the death of Messala from injuries he sustained during the race.

All during that time, Esther, the woman he loves, keeps telling Ben-Hur about Jesus, whom she has heard speak several times. This man wants people to love their enemies, she explains to Ben-Hur, but her words don't pierce him. It takes something Jesus Himself says on the cross to convince him. After Ben-Hur sees Jesus being crucified, he tells Esther, "Almost the moment He died, I heard Him say, 'Father, forgive them, for they know not what they do.' Even then . . . and I felt His voice take the sword out of my hand." And the hatred left him.

Why did Ben-Hur have to endure so many horrible situations before he was saved? For that matter, why do we sometimes go through terrible times? James tells us clearly: "My brethren, count it all joy when you fall into various trials, knowing that the testing of your faith produces patience.

But let patience have its perfect work, that you may be perfect and complete, lacking nothing" (James 1:2–4).

It's easy to have faith when things are smooth sailing and all is well. It's when everything comes crashing down on you, and your back is against the wall, that it's hard to remember to lean on Jesus. When you lose everything, will your faith stand strong? It's when we're at our very end that we find we must rely only on Christ and no one else. The writer of Hebrews tells us, "Without faith it is impossible to please Him, for he who comes to God must believe that He is, and that He is a rewarder of those who diligently seek Him" (Heb. 11:6). It is important not just that we have faith, but that we continually seek the Lord. It is then that He rewards us.

Let your personal actions show that, like Judah Ben-Hur, you have a stubborn faith.

## A PRAYER

Dear Lord, I desire the kind of faith where, in the middle of impossible situations, I have the confidence of knowing You are the way to peace and freedom. Please help me continually seek You. Amen.

## TAKE ACTION

- Be especially aware of your temper and bitterness this week. As you read Ephesians

4:31–32, pray for God's guidance as you try to put away these sins and embrace your faith instead.

- Train yourself to think in terms of mobilizing your faith to help you put away sin. To do that, you must make time every day to steep yourself in the Word of God. Determine when that will be, and start this week.

# 47

# Love

Travis, *Old Yeller*

> *"A new commandment I give to you, that*
> *you love one another; as I have loved you,*
> *that you also love one another."*
>
> —John 13:34

It is a tough time to be a man. It is just after the Civil War when the Coate family settles in Texas. They live the hardscrabble existence that settlers expect. In fact the only dollar the boys, Travis and young Arliss, have ever seen was a Confederate dollar bill. Travis is on the cusp of manhood, and when his father leaves to go on a cattle drive, Travis is determined to take care of his mother and little brother.

When he is plowing the cornfield on the very first day, a yellow streak barrels through, startling the mule so much it takes off, dragging the plow and tearing down fences as it goes by. Poor Travis is so angry at the yellow dog he wants to kill it. His mother tries to soothe him, but he throws rocks at the dog: "Git, you crazy, fool dog. Git! . . . I know one thing, that ole dog better not come around here while I got me a gun in my hands."

Arliss, on the other hand, loves the dog from the first, and he adopts it as his own, playing with it by the hour. Old Yeller, as he comes to be called, becomes Arliss's constant companion. One day the youngster gets ahold of a baby bear, and the mother bear comes charging at Arliss. And who saves him? Old Yeller, of course.

When wild pigs attack Travis, it is Old Yeller to the rescue again, drawing the pigs off of Travis and fighting them himself, both of them getting gored in the process. By this time, Travis and Old Yeller have formed a bond of love that is impossible to break. Travis, finding the injured dog, says, "Oh Yeller, Yeller. You're all cut to pieces. You're gonna be all right, ya hear? I'll get Mom. Mom'll fix you up for sure."

> "Git, you crazy, fool dog. Git! . . . I know one thing, that ole dog better not come around here while I got me a gun in my hands."
>
> **—TRAVIS COATE**

The family had been warned about "hydrophobia," or rabies, in the area, and they worry that Travis and Old Yeller might have caught it from the pigs, but Travis assures his mother that the pigs are not acting sick at all.

The boy and the dog heal up as good as new. Their luck

runs out soon, though, when Old Yeller defends Travis's mother and a visiting girl against a rabid wolf. "Lucky you had Old Yeller," Travis says to his mom.

"It was lucky for us, son. But it weren't lucky for Old Yeller."

"He's chewed up some, but he ain't bad hurt."

"No wolf in his right mind would have jumped us at the fire. That wolf was mad." She strokes Yeller. "I'll shoot him if you can't, but either way we've got it to do."

Travis loves the dog so much he can't end his life without giving him a chance, so he talks his mom into letting them keep the dog until he shows symptoms. Unfortunately, a month later, it is unmistakable: the dog has hydrophobia, and someone will have to put him out of his misery. It is Travis who loves the dog enough to shoot him and end his suffering. That heartbreaking day he takes a huge step toward becoming a man.

Travis loved Old Yeller as much as the dog loved him. Each of them put the other first—the dog by repeatedly rescuing the young man, Travis by taking on the dog's pain and putting an end to its suffering. This sacrificial love is what we're called to show each other. Jesus modeled it for us when He took on our sins and died on the cross. Why? Simply because He loved us. In John 13:34 Jesus says, "A new commandment I give to you, that you love one another; as I have loved you, that you also love one another."

By loving each other sacrificially, we honor Jesus and the price He paid for us. Do you show love toward others in your daily actions?

## A PRAYER

Lord, thank You for loving us enough to sacrifice Your Son for us. Please help me remember to show that love to others. Amen.

## TAKE ACTION

- Consider sponsoring a child at Compassion .com or WorldVision.org.
- Show love to God's creatures by spending some time volunteering at your local animal shelter.
- Write a note to someone special today and let that person know how much you appreciate him or her.

# 48
# Overcoming

Rocky Balboa, *Rocky*

> *Caleb quieted the people before Moses and
> said, "Let us go up at once and take possession,
> for we are well able to overcome it."*
>
> **—Numbers 13:30**

If you've seen the movie *Rocky*, you almost certainly remember him training for the big fight. In the now-famous scenes, Rocky pummels the sides of refrigerated beef hanging in the meat locker, jogs through his crumbling neighborhood and the Italian Market, sprints on the pier, and runs with arms upraised atop the stairs of the Philadelphia Museum of Art—all to that uplifting soundtrack. We feel triumphant right along with Rocky. And when he makes it to the final bell in his fifteen rounds against heavyweight champion Apollo Creed, we are exuberant, because we love to see an underdog accomplish something truly great.

What you may not know is that Sylvester Stallone was a

real-life underdog who had almost as hard a time as Rocky, fighting to get the movie made in the first place. It was 1975, and Stallone had hit pretty close to rock bottom. He had only $106 to his name, his car had just died, his wife was pregnant with their first child, and he had to sell his dog because he could not afford to feed him. After he wrote the script for *Rocky*, the studio didn't want him to star in it. They gave him a ludicrously low budget to film the movie, $1 million, which made casting a nightmare. They had to use friends and family members for some characters. Stallone wasn't a professional fighter; he was so clumsy he had a hard time hitting the speed bag. He got shin splints during the filming and broke a knuckle during the meat-locker scene. In short, he had a lot to overcome. The film, however, ended up triumphantly winning three Academy Awards that year.

In Moses' time there was a group of underdogs who also seemed to have everything stacked against them. The Israelites had been slaves in Egypt for four hundred years. Through an incredible series of miracles, God led them out of slavery, through the waters and the wilderness, finally to the promised land. It seemed they had it made when they were encamped just outside, ready to go in and claim the land God had promised them. They sent spies into the land to see what it held and who inhabited it, but only Caleb and Joshua came back with encouraging words. The rest of the men said the land was filled with giants, and described themselves as being "like grasshoppers in our own sight" (Num. 13:33).

The Israelites were so afraid that they wanted to go back to Egypt! And God was so angry with their lack of courage, He made them spend forty years, an entire generation, wandering through the desert before allowing them to enter the land flowing with milk and honey. But they persisted, and one day God led them in. They experienced victory after victory over the inhabitants of the land, until they stood strong in ownership.

Have you had a "Rocky" moment in your life, or perhaps you felt like a grasshopper against giants? This is nothing unexpected to God. He knows we will fail at times and falter in our faith, like the Israelites did. But you are precious to Him, and He has plans for you. Take heart! It's tempting to give up sometimes, but with His help, you can overcome your challenges and be as triumphant as Rocky.

Next time you feel as though you're facing an impossible army, remember that our Father provided abundantly for you for times just like this one. It's safe to lean into His promises and claim them.

## A PRAYER

Dear Jesus, at times I feel like I'm too small to accomplish anything. Please help me to overcome my fears and step out in faith. Thank You for helping me overcome the tough times. Amen.

## TAKE ACTION

- Read Judges 6–7, which tells about Gideon, a true underdog who defeated an army.
- If you feel like an underdog, remember that many, many of the heroes in the Bible—such as David, Moses, and Joseph—were underdogs when they started out too. Take one step today toward your goal, and God will bless your efforts as He did theirs.

# 49

# Self-Sacrifice

Harry Stamper, *Armageddon*

> *I beseech you therefore, brethren, by the*
> *mercies of God, that ye present your bodies*
> *a living sacrifice, holy, acceptable unto*
> *God, which is your reasonable service.*
>
> —**Romans 12:1** KJV

Bruce Willis wanted to die. To be more accurate, he wanted his character, Harry Stamper, to die in the film he was about to star in, *Armageddon*. The movie, about a gigantic asteroid that threatens to destroy all life on planet Earth, features a crew of tough oil well drillers led by the crusty Stamper. The US government asks them to fly through space to the asteroid, drill a hole eight hundred feet deep, and deposit a nuclear bomb in it to blow it apart.

Jerry Bruckheimer, the film's producer, went up to Willis's home to talk to him about the role. "We decided to cast him [Willis] in *Armageddon*; we flew up to his ranch.

I remember him saying to me, 'Jerry, just make sure if I do this part, the way it's written, the character dies at the end. Don't make him live. I want to make sure he dies.'"

Willis explained, "I really think I should die in this. I want to be that guy that stays on the asteroid and puts the jumper cables together and, you know, blows up the asteroid, doesn't make it back home."

Willis got his wish. At the end of the movie, the trigger control for the bomb breaks, and it has to be blown up manually. As the remaining crew take off to fly back home, the asteroid spectacularly blows up. You could hear the sobs in the theater as the audience realized that their hero had, indeed, died to save the world.

You don't have to be a Harry Stamper to be self-sacrificial. As we go about our lives, we often forget that we are to be living sacrifices daily for Christ. What does that mean? We must be willing to forget ourselves and commit to doing Christ's will in our lives. We are to love others as He first loved us, freely sacrificing our time and energy—even when we don't feel like it. That's how we honor Him and His sacrifice on our behalf.

## A PRAYER

Dear Lord, thank You for sending Your Son to die for us so that we can someday live with You in heaven. Please remind me that I live by Your grace. Amen.

# TAKE ACTION

- Most of us have memorized John 3:16, but read all of John 3 for the context of this well-known Bible verse about the ultimate self-sacrifice.
- If you haven't already, let your family know that you want to donate your organs in case something happens to you. You may give the gift of life to someone in need.
- Give willingly of your time to something your youth group or church group is doing this week, even if it's not your favorite activity. Perhaps it's visiting shut-ins or cooking for the homeless. Whatever it is, do it in a self-sacrificial and God-honoring way.

# 50
# Strong Will

Storm, *X-Men*

> *Like a city whose walls are broken through*
> *is a person who lacks self-control.*
>
> **—Proverbs 25:28** NIV

Since Storm first appeared in *Giant-Size X-Men* #1 in May 1975, she's been one of Marvel's most popular superheroes. Her mother was Princess N'Dare of Kenya; her father was American photojournalist David Munroe. Their daughter, Ororo (given the code name "Storm" by Professor Xavier later), was born in America, but the family moved to Egypt when she was a child.

This is where Ororo's life turns to tragedy; an airplane hits their house, and her parents are killed. The little girl is buried in the rubble with their dead bodies. Only she survives and crawls out of their demolished house, thereafter forced to live on the streets. As the young woman grows up, it becomes apparent she is a mutant, and she has some unusual powers.

It turns out Storm possesses

the psionic ability to manipulate weather patterns over limited areas. She can stimulate the creation of any form of precipitation such as rain or fog, generate winds in varying degrees of intensity up to and including hurricane force, raise or lower the humidity and temperature in her immediate vicinity, induce lightning and other electrical atmospheric phenomena, and disperse natural storms so as to create clear change. Storm can direct the path of certain atmospheric effects, such as bolts of lightning, with her hands. . . .

Storm's ability to manipulate the weather in her immediate vicinity is affected by her emotions; hence, if she does not maintain control, a fit of rage might induce a destructive storm.

Because she's had to practice control of the weather for many years, Ororo/Storm has a very strong will. Thus, like people who have power in the real world, she must maintain a strong will to prevent chaos and damage to others. In fact, one time, when she fails to control her powers, Storm almost creates another global ice age.

Do you know you have surprising powers too? With one word you can change a person's world. With one small action, you can affect the direction of someone's eternity. When you really put your mind and will to something, there's no end to what you can accomplish. What's the ability to whip up a storm compared to the power of influencing a life? Being strong-willed is just one of those gifts God gives us that we have to channel in a positive way, and then . . . look out!

> With one word you can change a person's world. With one small action you can affect the direction of someone's eternity.

However, when we lose our self-control, God says we are like a city whose walls are broken through. It leaves us vulnerable to all kinds of evil, unable to be a force for good in the world. We are of no use to God when we don't control our actions and our tongues. But we are not left alone to rebuild the walls to our city. God left us someone precious, the Holy Spirit, to guide us in our time of need. With Him you can be assured that you have Jesus with you as you build your self-control for His purposes.

## A PRAYER

Dear God, I know sometimes I'm strong-willed. Please help me direct that gift productively down the path that You would have me go. I know through You I can do amazing and positive things. Amen.

# TAKE ACTION

- Begin turning your negative instances of being strong-willed into positive ones. Instead of being indiscriminately "stubborn," decide to be strong-willed about standing up for the right thing, no matter what. Instead of giving off negative vibes or being pushy just for the sake of it, find a place people might be looking for a strong leader, or turn yourself to persistent prayer as in Luke 18:1–8.
- If you have a strong-willed child in your life, take a breath, thank God for that child's unique personality, and remember to appreciate what a great adult leader this child can grow to be.
- If you know that you have been strong-willed in a hurtful way in some area, cover it with prayer this week.

# 51

# Leadership

Rudolph the Red-Nosed Reindeer

*Blessed are those whose strength is in you.*

—Psalm 84:5 NIV

One of the most beloved Christmas carols started out life as an advertising gimmick! It's true. In 1939 Montgomery Ward tapped advertising exec Robert May to write a poem that their store Santa Claus could give away to children who came to visit him. "Rudolph the Red-Nosed Reindeer" first appeared in a little booklet published by the department store chain. More than 2.5 million copies were handed out. And by 1946 more than 6 million copies of the poem had been distributed.

Rudolph's story came to musical life in 1949 when May's brother-in-law, Johnny Marks, wrote the music. After it was turned down by Bing Crosby and Dinah Shore, singing cowboy Gene Autry recorded it. Today "Rudolph the Red-Nosed Reindeer" is the highest-selling Christmas carol, at more than 25 million units.

What makes this little carol so loved? Perhaps it's the pluckiness of the hero, Rudolph, who was the only reindeer never allowed to play any reindeer games. We can all relate to being rejected by our peers at some point in our adolescent years. Yet despite all the other available candidates, who did Santa turn to when the fog rolled in and the going got tough? That's right, the one with the shiny red nose, who was different from those who had once taunted him, the one with something special about him that was needed to accomplish the mission.

What makes this little carol so loved? Perhaps it's the pluckiness of the hero, Rudolph, who was the only reindeer never allowed to play any reindeer games.

"Won't you guide my sleigh tonight?" This is the point where many of us would be tempted to be small and mean, maybe even fearful, refusing to step up in leadership. But it's also the point where we hope we would have the heart of this little guy, accept the challenge, and allow ourselves to be harnessed in the lead. The psalmist said, "Blessed are those whose strength is in you."

It worked out well for Rudolph, with those other reindeer cheering him on, and if you are called to lead, with God's help, you can be a success too.

# A PRAYER

Dear Father, sometimes I feel like I don't measure up, and when I'm asked to lead in something, my instinct is to shrink away from it. Please help me remember that my strength is not my own, but instead comes from You, and guide me into the leadership role You may have for me. Amen.

# TAKE ACTION

- Has someone asked you to assume a leadership role, no matter how small? Try saying yes just once, and you'll discover new strength within.
- You may be called not to lead yourself, but to be one who encourages a leader. Find a leader in your life, whether in your family, your school, your community, or your church, and uplift that person in a special way.
- If you are in a position to, look for a child or a teenager who may be a little different from the rest and ask him or her to take a small leadership role. It's amazing to see the light go on in someone *else's* eyes when that person discovers he or she has value in *your* eyes.

# 52

# Thankfulness

George Bailey, *It's a Wonderful Life*

*And whatever you do in word or deed, do
all in the name of the Lord Jesus, giving
thanks to God the Father through Him.*

—Colossians 3:17

It's not often a fellow is thrilled to have a bloody lip, but
George Bailey was. The script says, "George touches his lips
with his tongue, wipes his mouth with his hand, laughs
happily. His rapture knows no bounds."

Of course, George is only happy because he's thankful to have his life back. Anyone who's ever seen *It's a
Wonderful Life*, starring Jimmy Stewart, will remember the
scene: George, who thought his life was worthless, has just
been shown what the town would be like if he'd never been
born. His faithful guardian angel, Clarence, has taken him
on a tour of the dismal place it would have been. No sweet
wife, Mary; no kids; no Bailey Building and Loan or the

homes it helped construct; no warm friends and good-hearted neighbors. No war-hero brother, since he had not been there to save him as a child. And now, now he has another chance. His lip is bleeding again, and the flower petals belonging to his little girl, Zuzu, are back in his pocket, proving to George that, yes, indeed, he has his life back.

Why, George is even happy to see the bank examiner—who has uncovered an $8,000 deficit at George's building and loan—a newspaper reporter, and the sheriff with a warrant for his arrest!

Off he runs, back home, past his wrecked car, past the sign for Bedford Falls, hollering, "Merry Christmas!" through the town center, the Bailey Building and Loan, even past the rotten Mr. Potter's office, where he pauses just long enough to call out, "Merry Christmas, Mr. Potter!"

At home the lights welcome him in; the Christmas tree is decorated brightly, presents underneath it. Why, George is even happy to see the bank examiner—who has uncovered an $8,000 deficit at George's building and loan—a newspaper reporter, and the sheriff with a warrant for his arrest!

"Have you seen my wife?" he asks happily.

Then he hears the voices of his children: "Merry Christmas, Daddy! Merry Christmas, Daddy!" they call to him, and rush to hug him, wearing their pajamas.

As Mary comes rushing in, out of breath, George shouts, "Hallelujah!"

"George! Darling!" she cries, and races into his arms. "Where have you been?"

George is thrilled to have his family back, but he has no idea what is coming next. The whole town has heard about the trouble and brought money in to make up for the deficit. Even his old friend Sam Wainwright arrives in time to cap it off.

The movie had started with prayers for George finding their way up to the angels in heaven.

> **GOWER'S VOICE:** I owe everything to George Bailey. Help him, dear Father.
>
> **MARTINI'S VOICE:** Joseph, Jesus, and Mary. Help my friend Mr. Bailey.
>
> **MRS. BAILEY'S VOICE:** Help my son George tonight.
>
> **BERT'S VOICE:** He never thinks about himself, God; that's why he's in trouble.
>
> **ERNIE'S VOICE:** George is a good guy. Give him a break, God.
>
> **MARY'S VOICE:** I love him, dear Lord. Watch over him tonight.
>
> **JANIE'S VOICE:** Please, God. Something's the matter with Daddy.
>
> **ZUZU'S VOICE:** Please bring Daddy back.

We can well imagine it ended with prayers of thanksgiving from the good people in Bedford Falls.

Frequently, when we pray, we're asking God for something. But how often do we remember to thank Him? Asking seems to come more naturally than thanking. But we are to be thankful to God in all things and to praise Him. Psalm 100 tells us to:

> *Enter into His gates with thanksgiving,*
> *And into His courts with praise.*
> *Be thankful to Him, and bless His name.*
> *For the Lord is good;*
> *His mercy is everlasting,*
> *And His truth endures to all generations. (vv. 4–5)*

Forgetting to be thankful can become a habit that sneaks in. This is just the kind of thing to which we are susceptible. If this is a struggle for you, confess it to the Lord and allow Him to guide your heart and your actions toward gratitude.

## A PRAYER

Thank You, Lord, for what You have blessed me with. Help me to be thankful in all circumstances and to remember that Your goodness is everlasting. Amen.

## TAKE ACTION

- Thank someone this week for something he or she has done for you in the past.
- Be on the lookout each day for something to be grateful to God for, and add this to your nightly prayers.

# Sources

Epigraph
John Eldredge, *Epic: The Story God Is Telling and the Role That Is Yours to Play* (Nashville: Thomas Nelson, 2004), 15.

Introduction
Rob Keyes, "The Avengers Breaks Second Weekend Record, Crosses $1 Billion," http://screenrant.com/avengers-box-office-second-weekend-billion-rob-171391/.

1. Justice: Superman
*Superman: The Movie*, directed by Richard Donner (1979; Burbank, CA: Warner Bros. Pictures, 2001), DVD.

2. Friendship: Mr. Spock and Captain Kirk, *Star Trek*
Memorable quotes for *Star Trek II: The Wrath of Khan*, IMDb, http://www.imdb.com/title/tt0084726/quotes.

3. Hope in Others: Belle, *Beauty and the Beast*
*Beauty and the Beast*, directed by Gary Trousdale and Kirk Wise (Burbank, CA: Walt Disney Pictures, 1991).

4. Mentoring: Mr. Miyagi, *The Karate Kid*
*The Karate Kid*, directed by John G. Avildsen (Los Angeles: Columbia Pictures, 1984).

5. Charity: Robin Hood
"The Gest of Robyn Hode," http://www.sacred-texts.com/neu/eng/child/ch117.htm.

6. Hope: Andy Dufresne, *The Shawshank Redemption*
SciFiScripts.com, http://www.scifiscripts.com/msol/Shaw/scenes_291
.htm.

7. Repentance: Eustace Scrubb, *The Chronicles of Narnia*
*The Chronicles of Narnia: The Voyage of the Dawn Treader*, directed by
Michael Apted (Los Angeles: 20th Century Fox, 2010).

8. Quiet Service: Alfred Pennyworth, Loyal Manservant to Batman
Michael Green, *Batman Confidential* #8 (October 2007).

9. Kindness: Melanie, *Gone with the Wind*
*Gone with the Wind*, directed by Victor Fleming and George Cukor
(MGM, 1939).

10. Tender Care: U.S. Marshal Reuben J. "Rooster" Cogburn, *True Grit*
*True Grit*, directed by Henry Hathaway (Hollywood: Paramount
Pictures, 1969).

11. Protectiveness: Katniss Everdeen, *The Hunger Games*
*The Hunger Games*, directed by Gary Ross (Santa Monica: Lionsgate,
2012).

12. Growth: Robin / Dick Grayson, *Batman Forever*
Molly Edmonds, "Are Teenage Brains Really Different from Adult
Brains?" Discovery Fit & Health, http://health.howstuffworks.com/
human-body/systems/nervous-system/teenage-brain1.htm.
*Batman Forever*, directed by Joel Schumacher (Burbank: Warner Bros.,
1994). All quotes are from the production draft of the screenplay
written by Akiva Goldsman, June 24, 1994, http://www.dailyscript
.com/scripts/batman_forever.html.

14. Truthfulness: Wonder Woman
*The Polygraph and Lie Detection* (Washington, D.C.: Board on
Behavioral, Cognitive, and Sensory Sciences, 2003), 295, http://
books.nap.edu/openbook.php?record_id=10420&page=295.

15. Faith in Others: Morpheus and Trinity, *The Matrix*
*The Matrix*, directed by Andy Wachowski and Larry Wachowski
(Burbank: Warner Bros., 1999).

16. Compassion: John Coffey, *The Green Mile*
    *The Green Mile*, directed by Frank Darabont (Burbank: Warner Bros., 1999).
    *Merriam-Webster Collegiate Dictionary*, 11th ed., s.v. "compassion."

17. Independence: Jane Eyre
    Charlotte Bronte, *Jane Eyre* (New York: New American Library, Signet, 1960), 318.

18. Integrity: Atticus Finch, *To Kill a Mockingbird*
    Harper Lee, *To Kill a Mockingbird* (New York: HarperCollins, 1960), 120.

19. Fearlessness: Indiana Jones, *Raiders of the Lost Ark*
    *Raiders of the Lost Ark*, directed by Steven Spielberg (Hollywood: Paramount, 1981).

20. Coolness Under Pressure: James Bond, *Goldfinger*
    *Goldfinger*, directed by Guy Hamilton (Beverly Hills: United Artists, 1964).

21. Protecting Others: Jake Sully, *Avatar*
    *Avatar*, directed by James Cameron (20th Century Fox, 2009). Quotes are from the screenplay: http://screenplayexplorer.com/wp-content/scripts/Avatar_screenplay.pdf.

22. Wisdom: Yoda, *Star Wars Episode V: The Empire Strikes Back*
    *Star Wars Episode V: The Empire Strikes Back*, directed by Irvin Kershner (Lucasfilm Ltd., 1980).

23. Intrepidness: Huckleberry Finn
    *The Adventures of Huck Finn*, directed by Stephen Sommers (Walt Disney Pictures, 1993).
    *Merriam-Webster Collegiate Dictionary*, 11th ed., s.v. "intrepid."

24. Honor: General Maximus Decimus Meridius, *Gladiator*
    *Gladiator*, directed by Ridley Scott (Dreamworks Pictures and Universal Pictures, 2000).

25. Determination: Ellen Ripley, *Aliens*
    *Aliens*, directed by James Cameron (20th Century Fox, 1986).

26. Encouragement: Woody, *Toy Story*
   *Toy Story*, directed by Jerry Lasseter (Emeryville, CA: Pixar Animation
   Studios, 1995).

27. Courage, Josephine March, *Little Women*
   Louisa May Alcott, *Little Women* (Rockville, MD: Serenity, 2009), 270.

28. Bearing Burdens: Samwise Gamgee, *The Lord of the Rings*
   "*Wikipedia*, s.v. Samwise Gamgee," http://en.wikipedia.org/wiki/
   Samwise_Gamgee.

29. Rising to the Occasion: Captain John H. Miller, *Saving Private Ryan*
   *Saving Private Ryan*, directed by Steven Spielberg (Dreamworks and
   Paramount Pictures, 1998).

30. Mastery: Zorro, *The Mask of Zorro*
   *The Mask of Zorro*, directed by Martin Campbell (Tristar Pictures, 1998).

32. Bravery: Dorothy, *The Wizard of Oz*
   *The Wizard of Oz*, directed by Victor Fleming (Metro-Goldwyn-Mayer,
   1939).

34. Gallantry: Sir Lancelot: *First Knight*
   Merriam-Webster.com, s.v. "gallantry," http://www.merriam-webster
   .com/dictionary/gallantry.
   "We're sorry, but Americans are becoming less polite," MSN Now, March
   15, 2012, http://now.msn.com/now/0315-americans-are-rude.aspx.

35. Putting Others Before Yourself: Sydney Carton
   and Charles Darnay, *A Tale of Two Cities*
   *A Tale of Two Cities* (London: James Nisbet, 1902) 183–84.

36. Teachability: Eliza Doolittle, *My Fair Lady*
   *My Fair Lady*, directed by George Cukor (Warner Bros., 1964).
   Edward Watke Jr., *The Lord Jesus Christ as the Great Teacher* (Revival
   in the Home Ministries, 2000), http://www.watke.org/resources/
   Christ_Teacher.pdf.

37. Forgiveness: Esmeralda, *The Hunchback of Notre Dame*
   Dustin Schledewitz, Bible Study 4U, http://www.biblestudyforyou.com/
   bible-study/forgiveness-devotional/.

38. Honesty: Sheriff Andy Taylor, *The Andy Griffith Show*
    "The Horse Trader," *The Andy Griffith Show*, season 1, episode 14,
        directed by Bob Sweeney (Desilu Studios, CBS Television Network,
        Paramount Productions). http://www.imdb.com/video/tvland/
        vi4150920217/.

39. Optimism: Don Quixote, *Man of La Mancha*
    *Merriam-Webster.com*, s.v. "quixotic," http://www.merriam-webster
        .com/dictionary/quixotic.

40. Responsibility: Spider-Man
    SermonIndex.net, A. W. Tozer, "Accepting Personal Responsibility,"
        http://www.sermonindex.net/modules/articles/index
        .php?view=article&aid=5469.

41. Relentlessness: Marlin, Nemo's Dad, *Finding Nemo*
    "Blue Marlin," *National Geographic*, http://animals.nationalgeographic
        .com/animals/fish/blue-marlin/.
    *Finding Nemo*, directed by Andrew Stanton (Walt Disney/Pixar, 2003).

43. Faithfulness: Nathaniel, *The Last of the Mohicans*
    *The Last of the Mohicans*, directed by Michael Mann (Warner Bros./20th
        Century Fox, 1992).

44. Duty: Horatio Hornblower, *Captain Horatio Hornblower*
    *Captain Horatio Hornblower*, directed by Raoul Walsh (Warner Bros.,
        1951).

46. Faith in God: Judah Ben-Hur, *Ben-Hur*
    *Ben-Hur*, directed by William Wyler (Metro-Goldwyn-Mayer, 1959).

47. Love: Travis, *Old Yeller*
    *Old Yeller*, directed by Robert Stevenson (Walt Disney, 1957).

48. Overcoming: Rocky Balboa, *Rocky*
    Chris Nashawaty, EW.com, "The Right Hook: How 'Rocky' Nabbed
        Best Picture," February 19, 2002, http://www.ew.com/ew/
        article/0,,203553,00.html.
    Sylvester Stallone, "The making of 'Rocky,'" ESPN Page 2, http://espn
        .go.com/page2/s/stallone/011207.html.

49. Self-Sacrifice: Harry Stamper, *Armageddon*

*Biography*, interview with Jerry Bruckheimer and Bruce Willis, "Bruce Willis," original air date October 7, 2001.

50. Strong Will: Storm, *X-Men*

"Storm-Ororo Munroe," World of Black Heroes, http://worldofblackheroes.com/2011/08/02/storm-ororo-munroe/.Comicbookdb.com: Comic Book Database, "Storm Marvel," http://comicbookdb.com/character.php?ID=173.

51. Leadership: Rudolph the Red-Nosed Reindeer

Kerri Carpenter, Children's TV @ Suite 101, "Rudolph & Robert: Robert L. May's Beloved Red-Nosed Christmas Reindeer," http://suite101.com/article/rudolph-robert-a175723, accessed June 2, 2012.

Kenneth T. Jackson, Karen Markoe, Arnie Markoe, *The Scribner Encyclopedia of American Lives* (New York: Simon and Schuster, 1998), 28.

52. Thankfulness: George Bailey, *It's a Wonderful Life*

*It's a Wonderful Life*, directed by Frank Capra (Liberty Films, 1946).